MORALITY FOR OUR TIME   MARC ORAISON

For all who rely on works of the law are under a curse; for it is written, "Cursed be every one who does not abide by all things written in the book of the law, and do them." Now it is evident that no man is justified before God by the law; for "He who through faith is righteous shall live."

Galatians 3, 10-11

MORALITY
FOR OUR TIME

Marc Oraison

Translated by Nels Challe

1968
DOUBLEDAY & COMPANY, INC., GARDEN CITY, NEW YORK

THIS BOOK CONTAINS

8

A NOTE TO THE READER

The following pages are no more than a tentative effort to articulate some of my own personal observations. If I were asked how they came to be written, I would be inclined to recount an incident that I can still recall quite vividly. One evening, in 1946 or 1947, I am not sure of the exact date, several of my colleagues in the school of theology and I were arguing the relative merits of a particular course in moral theology. On one point, at least, we agreed: each of us was profoundly disillusioned. Compared to what was being read in our biblical and dogmatic courses, the material was wholly unsatisfactory—and our professor admitted as much. As far as we were concerned, moral theology had been cut off from its vital sources and it was about time for a radical revision.

That was long ago. Since then I have had the opportunity to study and eventually practice clinical psychology. I came to share the excitement aroused in many others for the vast new areas of knowledge and reflection made available through Sigmund Freud. I more than suspect that the same excitement and consequent reflection have prompted this modest book.

For some while now a number of very prominent historians, theologians and exegetes have been pushing for reform in order to effect the renaissance in Christian morality we have all long awaited. It should suffice to recommend in particular the contributions of Bernard Häring, one of the most highly regarded representatives of the renewal movement. I am also prompted to mention a little book by F. Bourdeau and A. Danet entitled *Intro-*

duction à la Loi du Christ, which was published by Editions Ligel.

Throughout my own exposition I have been acutely aware of the contributions that have already been made, even though I refrain from mentioning them explicitly. I say this because I would be the first to admit that my remarks are predominantly based on clinical experience and reflection. My book was never intended as a commentary on other people's writings; it merely tries to introduce into the discussion the pertinent insights of psychological science. Yet I am amazed to see how often scientists and theologians arrive at identical conclusions despite the fact that their respective disciplines pursue their goals along quite different lines.

What you are about to read is unassuming and fragmentary. And undoubtedly you will find it disappointing. I will, however, say this: our age is on the threshold of an era of considerable progress. And a systematic effort of many specialists working in concert will be necessary to complete the work. In the meantime everyone has to apply himself to his own particular task as best he can.

MARC ORAISON

INTRODUCTION

It has become a truism that the twentieth century is character-ized by the accession of psychology to a role of eminent influence. A genuine revolution is afoot, beyond a shadow of a doubt; the very nature of human reality—your reality and mine—is being subjected to profound scrutiny.

In a manner not directly clinical or medical, contemporary phi-losophy, too, particularly phenomenology, is doing its part to alter radically our way of thinking. I for one am convinced that we are witnessing a moment in the evolution of the spirit no less extraordi-nary than the grand achievement of the thirteenth century or the profound crisis of the Renaissance. But because we are, willy-nilly, wholly implicated in the process, we are bound to find it extremely difficult to stand off and analyze it dispassionately. We are hard put to understand it in its correct perspective, much less to define its definitive place in human history. It is always intoxicating—or frightful—to participate in what Péguy refers to as "epochs," when something is taking place, as opposed to "periods," when nothing happens.

I think it fair to say that Western Man of the sixteenth century came to appreciate his own importance in reacting against that decadent and dogmatic brand of scholasticism which had betrayed the thought of Thomas Aquinas. Rabelais in this regard provides us with a rigorous and surely sympathetic example. In some way renewing contact with the cultures of antiquity reinstilled in hu-man reason a consciousness of its rights, faced as it was with the rigid and sterile, almost dictatorial, academicism of the period.

Now in the twentieth century, Western Man is faced with a restoration that is decidedly more difficult. Psychology and modern philosophy oblige him—and not without jeopardy—to recapture a far more lucid sense of his mystery and his apparently hopeless contradictions. We are not far removed from a generation that believed in constructing an ideal world answering to precise and definitive norms, the same generation which gave blind credence to the mythological "man of reason" who was to be sole master of himself. But witness: it was none other than man himself who razed the myth and modern psychology was perhaps the principal wrecking implement. We are discovering within our inmost recesses still unexplored regions that, far from holding their peace, are urgent in their anguish. They are mysterious in their apparent autonomy, and they abrogate the sweet rationalistic security that sustained us until now.

I will be the first to admit that this description is crassly oversimplified. But to my mind it expresses the essence of what is taking place. The violent reactions against Freudian psychology are an unequivocal sign of our times. We are awakening, often quite brutally, to the fact that we are not seldom the dupes of an unsatisfactory infancy. Whereas we feel that we are the convinced "masters of ourselves and the universe," in point of fact and quite unbeknown to us many of our actions are the product of our weaning and the encounters we had with our parents when we were no more than five years old. A very disagreeable discovery indeed! But if it is true we have the obligation to rethink *everything*, to leave no stone unturned, while by the same token holding fast to *everything* that is certain. This includes both science and the word of God. If we reflect, the task looks terrifying. And one can well understand why some people might feel inadequate to sustain the anguish and instead prefer to deny desperately or set aside what psychology has ascertained.

It is precisely with regard to morality that the conflict has become most intense. And understandably so, since here we are involved with more than a more or less adequate notion of ourselves: our entire sense of destiny is at stake. It is a very stark prospect to be compelled to choose between a "morality" that perforce participated in the prevailing rationalism of the last century and the blunt lucidness of our psychological disclosures.

Father Rimaud opened the discussion in no uncertain terms as early as 1949.[1] In the beginning the discussion is bound to be impassioned. Those who profess a doctrine solidly framed in abstract, irrefutable ratiocination see the psychologists as a menace to their emotional security. They have succeeded in reducing the fundamental anguish of human existence to a set of principles. But they will have to be shown that this resolves nothing. By ignoring our anguish it will only grow more intense and the defensive reaction will be charged with increasing aggressiveness and violence. Clinical psychologists can do nothing more than certify what they see and try to understand it. Their experience is based on certitude, in the best scientific and medical sense of the word. They ascertain, and subsequently try to demonstrate, that abstract reasoning[2] even when it is intellectually correct fails to correspond to the reality of life as it is lived. It is inadequate to resolve the existential problems of concrete persons and, in the last analysis, as an exclusive method of approaching the world it only constitutes an evasion of the issue. The aggressive opposition of the "moralists" in defending their own security only tends to evoke contempt. Nothing is so foolish as the denial of evidence, especially when it is obviously motivated by the defense of a number of preestablished "principles." We are surprised and shocked by the opposition marshalled against Galileo, because it clearly smacks of the mentality of the epoch in which he lived. But reaction against contemporary psychology is similar indeed. Whenever new discoveries challenge a conceptual system and its attendant verbal expression that is based on the mentality and knowledge of a bygone age, the systematic blindness of its defenders and their refusal to ask questions become especially irritating. The proponents of change appear to be in bad faith as viewed against the apparent sincerity of the opposition. But we generally fail to ap-

[1] "Les Psychologues contre la morale," in *Etudes* (Oct., 1949).
[2] The term is used here to indicate precisely the doctrinaire attitude, namely the affirmation of principles, but in ignorance of their existential ineffectiveness no matter how unquestionably "correct" they may be.

preciate that the opposition's righteous indignation is not of the scientific order at all. Consequently we find ourselves engaged in a "conversation of the deaf." Whatever it may be, it is certainly not dialogue.

Each party has in its possession a fragment of the truth, but the mutual refusal to consider each other's contribution eventually leads to insult. Thus we might overhear the two of them conversing—to their mutual loss:

> I tell you it's a horse!
> Well, I tell you it is white!
> etc.
> etc.

What kind of miracle will it take for them to realize they are both talking about a white horse?

As is always the case, such fruitless discussion has its roots in previous confusion. Some people object, "Psychoanalysis destroys morality." But in this case we have to specify what each of the key words actually designates. It is appalling to what extent the ignorant man will attack something simply because he does not understand it. But, after all, is he really capable of taking the trouble to understand? When we think of all the publications written on the subject, it is hard to appreciate how this kind of ignorance can still be inculpable.

I could go into exhaustive detail listing sundry aspects of the polemic. But I feel that in the last analysis they can be reduced to a few fundamental and very simple themes.

The moralists' principal attack gravitates around the elementary reproof: "You psychologists would abrogate sin." That is tantamount to saying psychologists destroy the notion of responsibility, hence the sanction and thus morality itself. Let me give a brief illustration: Peter is an alcoholic; psychoanalysts tell us he is conditioned to such behavior by an inferiority complex and seeks to compensate for his imagined deficiency by having recourse to artificial excitation. Does this mean that Peter is no longer culpable? What about sin? The moralist is terrified; this kind of thinking frustrates the organization of thought that underpins his life. Psychoanalysis, as a result, has to be an aberration because it denies the notion of freedom.

What the moralist fails to realize is that Peter is a sick person from the very outset, and no one can infer from the normal to the pathological. If it is anything, psychoanalysis is a therapeutic technique that appeals to whatever resources Peter has which will allow him to deliver himself from the unconscious affective condition that prompts him to drink. As a therapeutic technique it rests on scientific verification. But at the same time its fundamental presupposition, while neither articulated explicitly nor resting on some particular philosophical system, nonetheless is an implicit (and in some way absolute) belief in an unseen, unsuspected aspect of freedom within the individual. In helping the subject liberate himself, the obvious implication is a belief in his ability to become free, and a belief that by his very constitution he is free. The psychologist looks upon the psychological determinants as accidental fetters that restrain the freedom of his *sick* clients. Even if a psychoanalyst were to write volumes to demonstrate philosophically the non-existence of human liberty, when he takes up his position behind his reclining patient he is in effect affirming his belief in freedom. In fact the intensity of his affirmation might well confound the moralist: the psychoanalyst would not think of intervening in the mystery of his patient or influencing him in the slightest way. This is precisely why the psychoanalyst lets himself be psychoanalyzed periodically: to preserve his neutrality he wants to be as aware of his own personal motivations as possible.

Moralists should be aware that psychoanalysis "attacks" a neurotic personality disorder and nothing else. The patient's problem may have other dimensions; there is no implication in his behavior to the contrary. How Peter personally reacts to his behavior as an alcoholic, how he judges it, what references he has for his judgment—these are all considerations of a different order. During the course of therapy the psychoanalyst limits himself to destroying ruthlessly the *false* references and *false* judgments, the alibis that the sick person unconsciously imputes to himself. This does not mean that there are no *true* references; on the contrary, there are.

15

But determining just what they are is not the business of a technique that is first and foremost therapeutic.

It is not rare that a sick person concludes his therapy without having overcome his aberrant tendency. But he has reacted against it and is capable of making a judgment about it; he is capable of really suffering from it, of accepting that suffering and of enlarging the scope of his action. Once disengaged from a morbid and obsessional culpability, he is able to occupy himself with other facets of his person and to make genuine moral progress. But unfortunately the authentic complexity of human behavior does not register with the moralist, and he insists that psychoanalysis is just the opposite of what it actually is.

The other common reaction is an indignant, and always confused, protest against the "monster of immorality" that psychoanalysis finds lurking within the child. Modern psychology reputedly represents "that angel of purity and innocence" as a perverse polymorph. The moralist cries sacrilege, forgetting the while that he teaches elsewhere the universality of original sin. To insist that a three-year-old boy lusts after his mother and wishes the death of his father is enough to make one shudder. But the moralist who protests in this way usually neglects to inform himself as to what it all means. Consequently certain psychoanalytic formulations continue to lend themselves to ridicule and indignation.

What actually transpires within a child from the time he is born until he attains the use of reason cannot be adequately expressed. The child simply has not yet reached the stage where he is capable of clear conceptualization. The only alternative we have is to press into service certain adult expressions, knowing full well that they fail to convey the complete significance of the situation. When we say that a three-year-old child wishes the death of his father, we are right and we are wrong. If the psychoanalyst actually meant to imply that the child consciously and deliberately harbors homicidal intent, he would certainly have to prescribe incarceration. But obviously this is not what he means at all. Something very dramatic takes place within a child at this age due to his discovery that his parents belong to one another. The child reacts "as if" he wished the death of his father.

16

The expression "as if" occurs frequently in modern psychology. It indicates at once the analogous similarity and the distinction that exists between a child's interior events and our adult manner of expressing them.

Similar confusion is aroused when psychologists refer to infant sexuality, although it is nonetheless a fact. But while moralists are naturally predisposed to consider sexual morality from the adult point of view, they accuse psychology of viewing everything in the light of sex, not realizing that their own moral perspective is itself sex-centered. This is a classical instance of a curious but frequent paradox: we often impute to someone else something we do ourselves, albeit unconsciously, and then find we are unable to understand what the other person has to say.

Psychologists find it hard to refrain from a little reacting of their own. They see certain kinds of "morality" as disguising the deeper wish to dismiss morality altogether.

It can be averred that moralists have no criterion other than the law, and psychologists, since they reject constraint, are looking for some other criterion more in line with their clinical findings. That is exactly what we propose to do in this book. We harbor no illusions that we will resolve the debate of a sudden—that will take much work and involve a more concerted effort. But now, we feel, is the time to begin. Flight is not the answer. As we already mentioned we are in the midst of a revolution, and whether we like it or not that revolution continues to spread. Modern psychology, the viable issue of Freud's initial discoveries (which we call "clinical" or "dynamic" psychology), continues to clarify and transform all aspects of human relations: medicine, social service, the management of human enterprise, conjugal community, etc. The revolution announced by Karl Stern is leading inexorably to a more or less brutal confrontation between different conceptions of morality.

The initial results indicate that the shock is obviously a healthy one. Christian morality will emerge from the debate lucid and alive—but only on condition that it returns to being truly Christian. The current upheaval will give Christian moralists a chance to reflect upon the unique message entrusted to their care.

17

There is a revolution, then. But is it a revolution in morality itself? I think not. Instead it is a revolution pertaining to a conceptual construct (and its verbal articulation) that has gradually deviated from its original meaning and has thus become inadequate. Far from destroying morality, it should result in a more profound penetration into the significance and orientation of human behavior. I am not alone in this conviction.

I. MAN AND MORALITY

CHAPTER ONE: *What Is Morality?*

Ultimate achievement for any philosophy is found in a theory of morality. A philosophy that disregards the dynamics of human behavior in its conception of the world is patently deficient. For morality does more than add the final intellectual fillip to a particular philosophical enterprise; it implements it concretely and brings about its practical effect. This perhaps explains why we tend to judge the sagacity of a philosopher on the strength of his moral preachments. It is at once the summation of his thought and its crowning achievement.

Morality is, and has always been, the most crucial element in human life. Therefore it is all the more disconcerting to see how much uncertainty persists despite man's continued preoccupation with disclosing practical norms by which to order his conduct. A number of basic intuitions are common to most civilizations and philosophical systems—respect for life, a sense of propriety and justice, a concern for social order to preserve human existence— but they always assume a variety of peculiar forms. Sometimes in fact the basic intuition is barely recognizable within certain doctrinal systems. Even something so basic as the respect for human life with its associate inalienable rights rarely appears outside a discriminating context. Pagan civilizations denied the human dignity of slaves and barbarians; capitalistic cultures implicitly impugn the human dignity of proletarians, while Marxists do just the opposite.

Man has always been concerned with his predicament; he is preoccupied with comprehending the significance of the world and his human presence within it. Of the numerous definitions of morality that have been advanced, I would choose the one formu-

21

lated by Antonin Sertillanges: "Morality is the science of what man ought to be by reason of what he is."

Morality is first of all a science, though obviously not in the mathematical sense and not in the sense of the "exact (natural) sciences." Living as we do in a world dominated by the physical sciences, our notion of "science" has become somewhat limited, and perhaps unavoidably so. But for our present context we would have science understood as the aggregate of all conscious and established knowledge. Thus for instance when I go to the trouble of informing myself about the life, personality and peculiar habits of Napoleon, I feel I have acquired a science, though admittedly neither my term "science" nor my method have anything to do with the physical sciences. I note that this undertaking helps me to know Napoleon and to know myself at the same time, if only by the instinctive process of imagining myself in his place or in the position of the underling whose ear he pinched.

Every step in knowledge is simultaneously a step in the knowledge of oneself; each new confrontation with what is not myself represents and implies a personal meeting and an attitude that only I could know exists. This attitude could very well end in a refusal to confront myself any longer or in flight from existential engagement. In this event I can take refuge in universal and abstract ideas which permit me the reassuring comfort of a broad logic. A rationalistic or idealistic attitude of this sort involves far less personal jeopardy. It is less dangerous to sit at one's desk making logical deductions about volcanoes than exploring them firsthand. But even if I choose the less precarious pastime, someone still must leave his armchair and eventually tell me about his experiences. For all science is one. Even if the theoretician in his study should reject and hold in contempt the enlightened man who went in search of experience, he is totally dependent upon him. That is why I feel it anything but useless to keep recalling these two aspects of the scientific attitude: it involves a progression in the knowledge of oneself, and it affirms the fundamental primacy of human intercommunication.

Morality is a science. It is necessary knowledge. Paradoxically, we can define a man by means of the experience he has of himself.

In his relations with others man has the need to know. Without knowledge he does not exist at all; he disappears from the face of the earth. It is quite likely that man requires knowledge more than food. With an animal it is just the opposite. It has no need of knowing or, rather, of comprehending; everything happens as if it were known beforehand. Its behavior is wholly directed by what we call instinct. There is no distance at all between the animal and the world of which he is a part and an expression. He is one of the rhythms written into nature. Having no need to confront nature, he need not know himself. Self-consciousness and growth in understanding, which are inseparable, are basically two expressions of the uncertain and uncomfortable human situation. Therefore, there is no question of morality on the animal level. But for human beings totally disarmed upon arrival in the world, with poor reflexes of adaptation, restrained and so powerless, it is imperative to learn, to grasp and to understand, and thus to engage ourselves, which is the same thing.

But just as certainly the universal importance of morality stems precisely from the fact that it is not and cannot be an intellectual science; it is at its very core a "living science"—we cannot live without it.

Sertillanges calls it "the science of what man ought to be." We are projected irresistibly toward a future not yet fully realized. I am not yet fully myself, since there is a tomorrow and I do not know what or whom I will see; I am not sure I am going to wake up tomorrow in good spirits nor am I sure the day will be a pleasant one. Certainly I can foresee a number of things, but I do not know today how I will be tomorrow. I do not know quite who I will be tomorrow—myself to be sure, but a self I have still to discover.

It belongs to me to be me. Tomorrow's confrontation is bound to be new, even if it happens to appear monotonous. The same bus driver I meet each day on the way to the office will not be quite the same. His wife might have given birth to a son last evening or he might be angry with his best friend. Who will I be when I meet this man who is the same and yet not the same? This constantly new adaptation cannot be arranged in advance, or by habit. There always remains a margin of the unforeseen to guarantee that I always have the initiative in my personal attitude and comportment. I can rely on a mechanical set of gestures, words and practiced reactions to protect myself to some measure against the unknown, that is to say against life. But only to a degree. Life, complex and rich as it is, makes fresh demands on me each succeeding day, in spite of all appearances to the contrary. When "I" respond I will already have lived today and yesterday and the day before. I will already possess a certain experience of the world and of myself. For me, tomorrow will be entirely new and yet not new at all. And how am I going to respond? This is a question I have to ask myself at the very outset.

Obviously I can walk away from it or retreat into myself. I can dismiss the question of tomorrow's world or, for that matter, even today's. If I take the bus to my office, I can pretend to respond, without actually consenting to "be there." No one can act my part for me. If tomorrow I refuse to be what the day demands, I am the one who is going to suffer. I will have the bitter feeling of being less than myself; I will have failed to be myself to the extent I was not present to the world that interrogates me by its very presence. The imperative dictating what each person should be is not of some obscure order; it is at once the individual, irresistible appeal of the world and an exigency of my own proper existence. It is a call to constant discovery and progression; it requires movement, not stagnation.

"The science of what man ought to be by reason of what he is." First of all we must know who we ourselves are. This knowledge should be as accurate as possible so as not to unfavorably prejudice our knowing progressively more about ourselves in the future. If we devise or deduce things about ourselves on the basis of insufficient or false evidence, we are only inviting disaster.

DETERMINING AUTHENTIC MORAL NORMS

It should be clear from the beginning that we are investigating the problem in Christian perspective. We take for granted a world where someone other than ourselves knows the final word, who in revealing his own intimate secrets makes us known to ourselves. This divine revelation by no means dispenses us from personal reflection and quest. On the contrary, we might say it actually invites us to use our own initiative.

Now, aside from revelation the two ways of knowing ourselves and the world are science and philosophy; they represent the human spirit acting under its own power. And it is on this level that an authentic twentieth-century revolution is in progress.

The roots of the uprising can be traced far into the past, but particularly to the eighteenth century when for the first time man developed an authentic scientific attitude. There were of course prior attempts; we need only mention the contributions of the first Greek philosophers, Aristotle and the revival of research in the twelfth and sixteenth centuries. But it is only rather recently that we learned to disengage ourselves sufficiently from a "magical" mentality to the point where we are to make rapid progress in scientific knowledge of the world. Despite this advance, quite obviously we have neglected to investigate man himself in a similarly scientific manner. There has been unequal development in man's knowledge of the material universe on the one hand and what might be called a scientific knowledge of man-by-himself on the other. Symptomatic of that failure is the current unrest in the field of medicine.

It is certainly true that this relatively recent enterprise is more difficult than anything that preceded it, but then self-reflection was never very assuring. Science has progressed outward rather than inward, indicating that perhaps we are afraid of what we might discover about ourselves under sharp, methodical scrutiny. It has all the indications of terror in face of the inexplicable.

On the other hand, in the last ten years we have initiated an era of extraordinary development within the human sciences with the aid of Freud's radical transformation of psychology. It is not unlike the stimulus given biology by the discoveries of Pasteur. Formerly, psychology was looked upon as a part of philosophical or literary empirical knowledge. But now it has become a methodical and rigorous science, solidly established and rich in promise.

25

But while we have made a considerable leap forward in methodical reflection upon ourselves as personal and social subjects, psychology and psychosociology require us to pursue our reflection further. It is now a question of scrutinizing our own intimate selves, myself, you, our parents and our close friends.

At first glance this might be disconcerting or even frightful to some. But by virtue of the elementary principle that the revelation of God does not fail and that certain knowledge cannot be contradictory, these developments can only herald a better understanding of what God is telling us.

Along with psychology contemporary philosophy has also taken a new turn. The philosophical man of the twentieth century senses —sometimes vaguely, sometimes profoundly—that he is a captive of ready-made ideas and intellectual constructs whose foundations are no longer intelligible. He feels compelled to relive personally the reflection on life and the world, but first he must understand what is going on within himself. This does not imply that the intellectual constructs are devaluated in any way or, worse, that they must be destroyed—even if it may sometimes appear that way. The phenomenologist simply insists upon an experience of the world which is at once existential, lived and reflexive. His attitude precludes passing over thorny questions about a very complex reality that a philosopher of another bent might miss for love of correct but deceptive abstraction. There is a profound need better to understand what *exists*. We have to end the game played with purely intellectual concepts and cease contenting ourselves with philosophical questions that have no answers. I believe that in our concrete world of concrete realities this phenomenological endeavor is making an effort to arrive at the same clear verification as modern psychological research. The two disciplines have many points in common.

By way of summary, there are two ways of knowing what we are in order to become ourselves: the word of God and the actual state of our self-reflection (anthropology).

1. *Revelation*

Christianity is no more a philosophy than it is a morality. It is a religion. For man's part it represents the acceptance and integration of a living relationship with someone else (God). It is not at all simply knowing of his existence intellectually, but knowing him in reciprocal *engagement,* that is to say in dialogue.

If I am in someone's office in his absence, I can certainly discover something about him: I know he exists; I can ascertain what tobacco he smokes, what books he reads, his main line of work, his tastes, and perhaps even his height, age and manners. But I still cannot say that I know him until he enters the room and speaks to me. He first has to initiate a dialogue and solicit my response. This image expresses the difference between philosophical reflection about God and true religion.

A personal meeting which dispenses with abstract ideas (however correct they may be) is obviously going to change our perspective radically. It will singularly enlighten me and complete my knowledge of the person, of the room, of the inexpressible things about our lives, of myself and what takes place between us. In other words, to transpose the image, the incursion of God into our world by his direct word will precipitate profound reverberations in human reflection (philosophy) and in the behavior of men (morality). But nonetheless the very essence of Christianity—and we cannot stress this enough—is the real historical encounter.

A second comparison might help. The moment a man meets the woman he is to marry, he is somehow altered, yet retains the same identity as before. He is at once more free and more constrained. In the beckoning glance of the other he discovers his own personal meaning. And through a new, dynamic reflection he transforms his behavior for her sake and for the sake of their new relationship. Through an interplay of intellectual and existential knowledge the relationship assumes a distinct form. When the other is not physically present he is present in thought and his existence is taken into account. From what his partner already knows she attempts to deduce a deeper and more exact knowledge of herself, her beloved, and their mutual relationship. But once they are in each other's presence, this petty game of deductions gives way to more profound and literally unutterable truth. Ideas and words no longer suffice; the signs and symbols have evoked a mutual existential need.

Our living relationship with God, which is to say our religion, unfolds in an analogous manner: God was once present to us visibly in his historical incarnation, and now he is visible in the Church, but no longer in the manner of ordinary human beings. Therefore the sacraments as signs must be able to signify God and actually contain the real power of his presence.

It is an historical fact that mankind actually encountered God living and speaking, in the same concrete fashion as the couple we just mentioned. In fact the bible, and especially the prophet Ezekiel, uses the image of lover and beloved to illustrate its message. The entire history of the world is viewed as an ongoing dialogue. Abraham, Christ and the Church are accessible references in a comprehensive historical reality.

Seen in this same light the human situation is that of man being called by another to cooperate in accomplishing an exalted work. This is the significance of the first two chapters of Genesis. In the quintessential act of creation the Word called forth the human couple as a response. It was unlike any response that preceded it. Up until that moment the Word "commanded" things to exist; it was a world of inert matter, vegetation and animal life. The Word did not address himself to it. But the Word *spoke* to the human couple: "Be fruitful and multiply, and fill the earth and subdue it." In other words: Now it is your turn to act; we have something to do together. I am not speaking as a potter to a vase, nor as a woodsman to a tree, but to my son, my very own issue.

The human race is called by infinite love to a role of response; in fact it is an exigency of his very existence. Hence within the human race itself there must be mutual and intersubjective call and response.

Creation can be described as the first harmony of consciences; and it is at this moment that God made his initial call. The human race faced itself, lost interior contact with the presence of God and thereby transformed the harmony of the first morning to cacophony.

This is the mystery of dissociation. Notwithstanding, God pursued the dialogue along other lines so magnificently described in the Song of Solomon. And what is the whole of Hebrew history if not a witness to God's continual intrusion into ongoing events so as to make himself more intimately known? The definitive encounter is achieved finally in Christ. Henceforth the human race succeeds in finding itself in him and through him at the very moment of his apparent failure. This is a much more profound harmony, since it involves a unique call that actually alters our very form.

Thus God (himself a threefold subject) addresses individual men of all races as so many subjects by means of an infinite exchange of love across time. First and foremost the Christian is a resurrected person. He is conscious and ongoing. Whatever he does he will not refuse or oppose God.

Consequently the moral law is simply an indicator; it reveals (to use St. Paul's phrase) a sense of our own drama, namely the necessity to love.

2. Anthropology

Anthropology has made significant advances in the last sixty years. We have become less and less preoccupied with man in the abstract and have learned to direct our investigations toward man as he really exists. At long last we are subjecting the human presence in the world (as both individual and collective) to the rigors of scientific study. And not without effect. Several broad lines are already converging, as if inviting us to draw some proper distinctions and to attempt an initial exposition.

As propitious as the occasion might be, the task is still a difficult one. We have to deal with dimensions and perspectives of truly novel character, and our vocabularies offer us no appreciable assistance in giving expression to what we see. If we want to avoid the technical jargon that is unintelligible to non-specialists, all we have left at our disposal are words that already have been used to describe other things and, consequently, are tainted with alien cultural significance. Anyone bent on studying modern anthropology goes into the field like an explorer trekking uncharted terrain. There are only hints of paths, and settlements are few and far between.

One of the fundamental affirmations of this new discipline is the psychosomatic unity of the individual human subject and his ultimate uniqueness. There is no "body" or "soul" to serve as container and contents. Psychic life at all its stages is expressed on the somatic register as much as in self-consciousness. In fact the impact of affectivity on the biological mechanism appears much more crucial than the reverse process. Just as it is arbitrary and false to dissociate the sun from its rays, it is unpermissible to *separate* the body from the soul—something quite different from distinguishing between them. While this observation is based on clinical evidence and methodical investigation, even Thomas Aquinas, who only had philosophical reasoning at his disposal, was able to arrive at an identical conclusion regarding the unity of the human person. There is not "my soul" and "my body"; there is only myself. Unfortunately, however, our entire vocabulary gravitates around the dualistic notion that anthropology no longer finds acceptable.

When Francis of Assisi referred to the source of his bodily deficiencies as "my brother ass," he was unable to express in other terms what he actually meant. And today his image has no contemporary significance, except perhaps as a vestige of an outmoded mentality. When we say an ascetic has become the "master of his body" (and I grant this might involve pathological aberrations), we are not particularly concerned with his body as such, but rather with certain affective forces which are expressed bodily and emotionally. When St. Paul speaks of the "flesh," we are not supposed to understand the body in the organic sense as opposed to some more-or-less ethereal "spirit." The dualistic notion is dangerous insofar as it distorts the profound sense of God's inspired message and effects a regression to an archaic, pagan mentality. If we want to do justice to the integral context of Pauline thought, the "flesh" has to be understood as the "carnal condition" involving the

30

mysterious contradiction of sin. And sin is an attitude of man's spirit, not his physiological organism.

But if the human condition characteristically involves an indissociable psychosomatic world then each individual reality, each concrete personality, is absolutely unique; it cannot be identified with any other personality, and in a sense it is *alone*, sometimes dramatically so. The contemporary theater (Ionesco, for instance) provides evidence to this effect in a paradoxical and tragicomic form; sometimes it is so charged with anguish that we mask it under a flood of pseudo-language and conventional conversation.

There is no need to belabor the clarification modern psychology gives of this attitude. The individual personality sets and elaborates itself from birth—if not earlier—in living relationships with the concrete personalities of its immediate surroundings. There is, for example, the "Oedipal" confrontation that occupies a moment of this long and obscure personal history. But the child does not enter relationships with an abstract mother and father, but with particular individuals, who are themselves the product of their own personal histories.

No two human beings have an identical history. Though a family gives every guarantee of stability, no two children will have lived the same moments of this stability, since it something in constant flux and always liable to be put in question. Ideal maturity can be described as the full assumption of one's personal solitude, "solitude" being understood here as a personal awareness that I am totally autonomous and distinct. This is man's sole mode of being: to live at a distance from others. Otherwise dialogue is impossible and, hence, existence itself. Up until a short while ago the notion of the "human person" was something purely metaphysical. Now it is being reevaluated in a new light: it is a unique and subjective existential reality that can only exist in an authentic sense when it enters into relationships with other individuals.

At this point I would like to cite an eminent psychoanalyst, Dr. Hesnard, one of the pioneers of modern psychology in France. He concludes the introduction to his book *Psychanalyse du lien interhumain* (Editions Presses Universitaires de France) with the following lines:

31

The human person is not . . . construed as mechanism or spirit. It is a being of flesh that is total and individual and cannot be understood except through the *bond* which unites it to its inter-human milieu. . . . When this being integrates the organic or biological activities that maintain its existence, and the bond it-self, with its biological milieu, it is called *body*. When it inte-grates, along with organic activities, its activities of need or affec-tivity, thus identifying itself with the objects of its vital interests and *binding* itself to other living human beings, it is called an individual. When it integrates, along with its organic and instinc-tive activities, activities of a complex structure, thus identifying itself as a self and with others like itself as a spiritual projection of some ideal, thereby becoming a value-conscious being, a being of rights and obligations that becomes more related to other men in its moral intimacy as it acquires autonomy and liberty, it is called a *person*.

After reading a statement like this one could hardly maintain that psychoanalysts deny or suppress human liberty!

In the same introduction Dr. Hesnard continues:

We also ascertain among civilized peoples the existence of a pro-found socialization that exerts its energy on natural intersubjectiv-ity for the purpose of human communion as this collective bond is further evolved.

This is not a purely philosophical gloss. Dr. Hesnard's theoreti-cal reflections are the product of long years of clinical experience. For the first time in human history man is investigating himself methodically; he is no longer dependent upon introspective intui-tion alone. He is taking note of the fact that he exists only by and for love, and he is prepared to use this ascertainment as a new basis for philosophical and religious reflection.

The human person in the reality of his existence does not engage in relationships with principles or with a law. He rather binds him-self to other *persons*. This constitutes the affirmation of the self as subject of intersubjectivity. This can occur at different levels; the clinical experience of the interhuman stage (whether it be preconscious or conscious) does not of itself exclude the existence of other stages.

To say "I" is to respond to another because that person by his "word" (and here we do not restrict the term to articulated language) posits me as subject. The child discovers himself as a subject in his relations to the parents who wanted him (or *accepted* him, which comes to the same thing). This self-discovery is very primitive; it is like seeing oneself in a mirror for the first time. One day through my parents' concern for me I came to understand that *I* was existing, and I laughed with joy. By the same token, one day through the concern shown me by the incarnate Word, I came to see that *I* was existing even more than I had thought, and death took on meaning.

It is no wonder that the dynamic character of the person that is cultivated in contemporary science has replaced the old, abstract notion of a static metaphysical entity. The human person is constantly on the go, encountering until death a variety of complex situations and individuals without ever being able to say his own structurization is complete. This constant forward movement is oriented toward effecting increasingly more successful encounters. As present-day psychological science sees it, man's natural destiny is to achieve that communion of which Hesnard speaks. If I may quote him again:

> Social psychology obliges us to characterize peoples and nations by an analysis of the psychic bond that draws men together into collectivities, large or small, open or closed. *Without this natural bond none of these groups could aspire—except very seldom—to universality, since they would certainly fail to realize it even in perfunctory fashion.*

THE DRAMA OF HUMAN BEHAVIOR

The italicized portion of Hesnard's last remarks are of singular importance. It is not only replete with meaning but it poses some important questions as well. Here Hesnard is introducing an aspect of anthropology that is extremely difficult to express and even more difficult to accept. It is what I would readily characterize as the "dramatic" aspect.

33

The history of any human being is in reality a tension, a fundamental dynamism of opening himself in order to recognize others and to be recognized by them in return—without his ever being entirely successful. Here some classical images are to the point: Man is chained to freedom and he eventually succeeds in realizing that the chains are deep within himself, so deep in fact that they elude his reach. This bears out the evidence of anthropology. Psychoanalysts understand only too well that even in an optimal case the best they can hope for is a *clinical* cure for the sick person. They only hope they can allow him to live in a more autonomous fashion relative to his own personal drama, the deepest sources of which remain inaccessible. Perhaps it is right here that psychoanalytic discoveries have precipitated the greatest shock. A rational and scientific—or, if you will, conformist—world is incapable of enduring such a revelation of the real mysteries of the human soul. It is never very agreeable to recall that we are not masterpieces that the maker has succeeded in forging to his own image and likeness. In fact some people react against the unpleasant reminder in a particularly violent manner. These are people who are couched in the false security that an inflexible way of thinking provides. It is not a matter of chance that medical doctors, ecclesiastics and mathematicians, to name but a few, reject the contributions of dynamic psychology with a vehemence closely akin to despair.

It goes without saying that their opposition should not keep us from articulating our recognition of man's drama and attempting to fathom certain of its aspects. At best the enlightenment proffered by modern psychology will only further underline the inaccessibility of a definitive explanation. Even if we do disclose certain aspects of the how of things, we are still left with a disturbing silence about the ultimate why, a silence that is the fault of none other than man himself.

The only value that develops without limit toward the infinite —a value that coincides with the person—is the encounter and communication between individual consciences. Everyday experience indicates that *authentic* encounters are rare and limited. *Total* intercommunication is impossible; I cannot communicate totally with another person because I am never totally *distinct* or *different* from him. In every encounter which engages me ever so minimally, I bring along my "interior world," a large part of which is unconscious. Practically speaking, it cannot be otherwise. Perfectly balanced as I may be, there are in me inaccessible balances of all my earliest affective experiences. Even before initiating a conversation with another, I have an "image" of him, a ready-made representation which is not a function of him at all, but rather of me. If this image remains in the background and interferes only marginally with the encounter, it will do no more than limit an otherwise fruitful dialogue. But if my preconceived image were unknowingly to take the upper hand, then dialogue would be impossible.

To clarify this admittedly oversimplified aspect of things, I would say that this "image of the other" exists simultaneously on two planes, only one of which is directly accessible to our consciousness.

At the outset there is what we could call the imaginative level. For example, I arrange a business meeting with a prospective client. I do not as yet know him; I have never seen him and know very little about him. Looking forward to the meeting, I "prepare" what I am going to say beforehand. But what invariably happens is that I *imagine* my client, his way of reacting, his bearing and his personality. I decide: "I will say this to him; and if he answers thus and so, I'll retort. . . ." This goes on and on, as a kind of rehearsal. This imaginary dialogue takes place in *me*, with a person I carry about inside me, after a manner, and whom I project. This imaginary man is created as a function of the person I happen to be, since I do not know my visitor sufficiently well to have even an approximate idea of him. I create *what I need him to be like*, either to obtain what I am after or to manifest some sort of aggression. When I face him in person, he is always completely different than I imagined he would be. If I let myself be duped by my imagination I run a risk of deceiving myself; we would begin our conversation badly, thereby jeopardizing any positive results that may have been forthcoming. But this is so common to one degree or another that all we can do is try to avoid the pitfall as much as possible.

This is rooted in an unconscious zone of our psychic apparatus that is the vital residue of our earliest affective experiences. From infancy the child creates progressively clearer notions of himself and others through his association with people who share his environment. The earliest encounters with the "non-self" are portals to our conscious reflections later on. If our affective development was normal, the unconscious interior world of "notions of the non-self" will not prejudice our adult relationships with reality. But there will always be a certain amount of inability to communicate: what I carry in me of my earliest experience is too subjective and too inaccessible to exploration to integrate it into my actual adult situation; it simply cannot be *verbalized*.

It often happens that in our encounters with other persons we try to reduce them to this primitive "vision of the world" which we carry about within us and which we find awakened in times of emotional stress. Some psychoanalysts regard this vision of the unconscious world as a "world of phantasms" in order to distinguish it from simple imaginary projections. In its extreme form it arouses a feeling of fear in the one so conceived, for it is a genuine menace to his unique existence. No doubt this explains the profound discomfort we feel in the company of "strangers" since, down deep, we sense that we "do not truly exist" for them. We experience authentic anguish when we are deprived of being ourselves.

Of course this is the pathological side of the situation. But it helps us grasp what takes place in various lesser degrees in every human situation. And if we take time to reflect, it will become apparent just how frequently this "world of phantasms" intervenes in human relationships to the detriment of all dialogue. It is precisely the insufficient perspective obtaining between two persons in each other's presence that prevents them from being wholly themselves. This is even true on the physical level. If I am too close to someone, I actually do not see him—the pores of his skin perhaps, but not *him*. And if I am too far away it goes without saying that I do not see him either.

Psychoanalysts who speak of the "world of phantasms" regard it as a fundamental tendency in all human encounters—even successful ones—unconsciously to view the other person in a thor-

oughly narcissistic manner. Mysteriously and primordially we identify him with ourselves, and by refusing to separate him from us
we find that we are unable to locate and identify him. If we could
resolve this enigma we would know liberation: to know the other
precisely as other would be to accept the fact that we are indeed
separate beings. But the enigma is an insoluble one; the ultimate
"separation" which would permit us to be *integrally* ourselves in
any encounter with the other is in all probability only realized in
death.

Within this web of confusion obscuring every personal encounter, "law" intrudes as an ambivalent imperative. Law obviously
indicates how I ought to behave if I am to establish successful relationships with myself and with others. But the primitive emotional factors involved in the moral entreaty can arouse my instinctive fear. "Law" always tends to wedge itself between the
other person and myself (and between me and myself) in order to
assist me in finding something I have lost. Consequently I run
the constant risk of using other persons to relocate that primordial
part of myself from which I really ought to dissociate myself.
Herein lies the impasse and illusion of legalism, at once so complete and despairing. It is in this sense that St. Paul speaks of the
"killing" power of the "law" (Rom. 7).

THE DIVINE PERSPECTIVE

In light of what we have seen of modern anthropology I think
it would at this point be profitable to recall rather succinctly several aspects of Judeo-Christian revelation.

What crowns and dominates this revelation is the God who
makes himself known as the *trinitarian mystery*, that is, as three
subjects so infinitely distinct and distant from one another that
they are infinitely one. Christ let this be known to his apostles
when he said: "If I do not leave the Spirit cannot come." For
love to establish itself in eternal perspective, the resurrected Christ
had to distance himself from sensible and temporal experience.

The existence of the universe, whose essentially dynamic, evolutionary character has been established by modern science, is the response to a call. As St. John relates in the preface to his Gospel, the spoken Word summoned the universe into existence and continues to sustain it. At the end of an enormous succession of created life, man, or rather the human couple, appeared at the apex of creation to empower that creation to actually *answer* God's call and not simply to obey it as had hitherto been the case. However, as a self-conscious creature man turned toward himself; he listened to himself and became deaf to the call of love. We might say that this reaction was typically "natural" for the human race in its first stage of self-consciousness, and now a new intervention became imperative to unify the race as well as to integrate each individual. At the first stage man was only beginning to establish interpersonal relationships. Due to its insufficiency the relationship was crude and still quite illusory. So God intervened in human history. A woman well schooled in her cultural heritage became so completely attentive to the divine call that the historical event actually took place inside her: the Word-made-flesh was conceived within her human *flesh* (in the integral, psychosomatic sense we were speaking of before).

He also came to break the bonds of death that had been established by the deadening of human conscience. The entirety of human history could now be unraveled in its full significance; the call of God went forth and brought into being its unique answer. Christ said: "He who believes in me has life . . . and I will raise him up on the last day." But, and this is clearly implied, we can *refuse* to believe in him; we can refuse to *see* him; we can refuse his word. There is no affirmation, I think, so strong and so concrete regarding human freedom. It is easy to understand why some people find the thought frightening: nothing is at once so simple and so difficult as to say Yes to someone.

Finally, using numerous images, the most frequent of which is the wedding banquet, Christ announced the kingdom of heaven as the perfected world he came to create. This is the network of interpersonal relationships established in perfect *communion* without the least trace of reticence. This is the vision that is able to dispel the somewhat bitter nostalgia we can sense in the writings of Dr. Hesnard.

It is worthwhile to recall St. John's mention of the "sin which leads to death" (1 Jn. 16): the personal rejection of the personal salvation that Christ earned for us by his blood. According to the transcendental logic of revelation, the refusal to be loved is what actually kills.

THE POINT AT ISSUE

Everything I have indicated up to now has been by way of introduction. I now want to address myself to the crucial issue.

Through the centuries the word of God—that other who is love —has been confused with elements of natural knowledge, natural reflection, natural expression. But at this particular stage of the revolution when man is becoming acutely aware of himself and his own drama, the rationalists' articulation of the word of God is ridiculous and tragic in its insufficiency. Now as in other great periods of the Church's history, theologians who want to transmit the word rather than to study in libraries have a grave obligation to remain faithful—or better, to deepen their fidelity—to the word of life. Since this will require illumination, no one in the twentieth century can afford to be satisfied with an oil lamp when he has electricity at his disposal.

Before we return to Sertillanges' definition of morality it is legitimate to ask whether or not a genuine moral revolution is in progress. And by this I mean a revolution in the way morality has been traditionally articulated. By now I think the reader is aware that my answer is an emphatic Yes. And if I were asked to describe quickly the nature of the revolution, I would say it entails a process of purgation. Traditional notions have congealed and become static and stultifying; consequently we are currently making every attempt to restore dynamism to moral thinking and to resuscitate our moribund conceptions of the world and man's relation to it. The only thing that might be surprising about the revolution is that it should come only now.

But when did it actually begin? What were some of its causes? I tend to think that the confusion in the post-Constantinian era between the earthly city and the kingdom of God is far from insignificant in this regard. I think we fail to appreciate the terrible slackening of spirit that was introduced by the theocratic government of the period. But then again neither is the tendency to revert back to that theocratic notion of political society about to disappear, since it represents a highly archaic regression toward the mentality of the primitive tribe passing from nomadic life to a stable society. But whatever the precise cause or causes, one thing is certain: the rise of moralism progressively obscured, paralyzed and falsified the Christian dynamics of behavior. Moral speculation gradually dissociated itself from the context of human acts and began to be bandied about by a closed group of professionals. In due time this led to the impasse modern psychology demonstrates to be intolerable.

Modern man is fundamentally dissatisfied with abstract principles that are rigorously deduced one from the other. Their inexorable character befits a Prometheus or Greek philosophy, but certainly not the message of the Gospel. The rationalistic structure in its entirety must be interrogated by the modern human sciences.

Any formulation of morality that is supposed to have a profound effect on our way of thinking has to be the result of a second, more perceptive look at the word of God and the true nature of human reality. It might well require several decades of concerted effort, but we have no choice. We either expend the energy and find collaborators or we suffer an irreparable loss. Now is the time to ask whether what we generally call "Christian morality" is in fact truly Christian; whether the "values of Christian civilization" that some people are prepared to defend to the death—without ever explaining what it is precisely that they understand by the phrase, I may add—are actually derived from Christ, or whether perhaps they are vestiges of an ancient Stoicism, or whether an adamant fidelity to certain traditions is not tantamount to betraying authentic Tradition, that is to say the life of the Spirit in the Church.

Among the many reflections by competent psychologists on the central problem of morality, I would like to single out for special mention a work by Dr. Berge, entitled *Les Maladies de la vertu* (Grasset, 1960). It poses the same question we do at the moment. And while admittedly it does not treat the problem in its theological context, it does provide a wealth of clinical evidence that we cannot afford to ignore. He writes: "We must all the same ask ourselves the question whether morality is made for man or man is made for morality." In effect he is asking whether we have understood that man has been created to achieve complete happiness (the very foundation of morality according to Aquinas) and not to be sacrificed to a body of drastically depersonalized teachings. Dr. Berge goes on: "A moralizing morality has made all morality suspect." As we see, psychologists are crying out against this obvious form of inhumanity. It is now up to theologians to examine whether our pretense at morality is not in effect the ultimate subtle refuge of a pride that actually misconstrues the existential relationship of man to God, the creator and savior.

CHAPTER TWO: *What Has Become of Morality?*

As soon as we get down to the business of serious reflection and are willing to entertain questions that might at first be disturbing, we are bound to be struck by the contrast between the findings of anthropology and the traditional formulas of morality. It is more than a contrast; the terms are incompatible. Modern psychology is not speculative; it is based on scientific observation and discloses real man engaged in a dramatic dynamism of existential relationships with other men and the world around him. On the other hand the traditional formulation of morality is a logical series of normative abstractions almost entirely extraneous to the human situation.

AN EXAMPLE OF A MORALISTIC FORMULA

The reader might find it difficult to grasp with sufficient force the stark opposition between the actual facts and the moralizing formula. Therefore the best thing to do is to open a significant volume and demonstrate our point. I have selected the French manual entitled *Théologie morale catholique* (Catholic Moral Theology). It is a classic in its field and is designed as a textbook for the professional student and as a reference work in solving what we ordinarily call difficult "cases." I must insist that it is of no mean reputation; on the contrary, it has been cited frequently and is still in use as of this writing. I have chosen it because it is a perfect illustration of what we nowadays call "Catholic morality," namely that morality which generally stifles the dynamics of human behavior. The arrangement of thought represented in this volume has not only influenced Christian morality, but morality in general, and sometimes quite markedly at that.

The reader is struck by the opening paragraph of the book. Under the title "Morality in General" an entire page is dedicated to the following text:

> Man must attain his last end by his *personal activity* in conformity with the remote (objective) rule and the proximate (subjective) rule of moral action, namely law and conscience respectively. These rules are violated by sin; their observance is facilitated by the virtues. From this the division of morality in general naturally stems.

While the manual pretends to expostulate Catholic moral *theology*, morality is defined without the least mention of God as an acting person. It conceives of human activity as independent of God's action. Before we even get into the book we find ourselves distracted from all revelation, from all mystery and theology. The Christian reader is apt to realize that this bodes ill for authentic religious reflection. He knows perfectly well that man will attain his last end by the grace of God, and yet as far as the manual is concerned nothing could be less to the point.

What happens to the fundamental notion of the drama of salvation in this perspective? What it has to say clearly contradicts St. Paul's epistles to the Galatians and the Romans where we read—and note that this is a matter of sacred scripture, a fundamental reference of our faith—it is neither the law nor its observance which saves. On the contrary, the law although good in itself actually kills. It is grace, that is to say love, that is our salvation. For the author of the manual the grace of Christ is of so little consequence in attaining man's ultimate end that he does not even mention it.

We could hardly imagine two positions more diametrically opposed, and we ought to be nonplussed, if not scandalized, that statements so obviously contrary to Christian revelation are not vigorously condemned by the Church.

44

Even if we only study this brief and clear text in reference to the findings of modern psychology, our reaction will be no milder. This is the kind of thing that makes such psychologists as Hesnard either worry in silence or protest. Man is being explicitly viewed as relative to two points of reference, the one abstract and the other subjective: law and conscience. In other words—and it is most important to understand this kind of reasoning—man is a solitary entity. The implicit affirmation is that he is an isolated individual who is only capable of living in relation to an abstract formula and himself. The other, our neighbor, can only be related to as an occasion or a pretext (a sort of "object event") that sets in motion the individual's reactions, good or bad, to the law and the "interior voice." The psychologist might think for a moment that he is being transported into a schizophrenic universe.

THE AUTHENTIC ROLE OF LAW

What does the law represent in the affective evolution of the human subject? Our answer requires that we take several considerations into account. Without going into exhaustive detail, we can say that for the child the law is first experienced as a prohibition coming from his parents and most especially from his father. In his still unorganized world, the child can be guided only by his initial experiences or through his education and training. He can live his first experiences in a world full of things that are "permitted" or "forbidden" without personal reflection or comprehension. He will not really be capable of comprehension until he is six or seven years old.

Here we have a reality that is exclusively affective and emotional. The infant reacts joyfully or fearfully at various levels to a confusing mixture of "formulas" that stem directly from the family atmosphere: habits, prejudices, conventions, true moral values, etc. The difficulty for the child consists in gradually establishing himself as a subject, that is, as responsible for himself in his encounters with other subjects who most immediately face him, namely his mother and his father. This is precisely where we locate the primordial importance of what psychology calls the Oedipal conflict.

Law is first experienced without a "human face," as a kind of absolute magic without personal reference. It is promulgated, ratified or sanctioned by the father, but the child has not as yet "met" the father as a "someone" before whom he can establish himself as another "someone." He will be unable to do this until he resolves this Oedipal crisis and until the experience of the archaic "law for itself" is resolved through intersubjective dialogue. Then the law will be experienced as the word of the father whom the child knows personally and with whom quite another sort of dialogue has been established. The father himself will appear as someone who submits to the law for his own good. The law will become a "meeting place" which is sought as a way of establishing satisfactory relationships with the other, who is eventually discovered and known as the final reference. But the difficulties in this passage are such that the adolescent, upset in his progress by the psychosomatic explosion of puberty, will for a time find himself making "legalistic" reflexes, often quite camouflaged, as an instinctive refuge for his primitive childish security. This proves that even the normal adolescent has not fully bypassed all his previous stages of development: he has not yet found the total security which will permit him to move forward without periodic regressions.

What is important then is that the child reach a stage of maturity sufficient to permit him to *command* his own behavior *spontaneously and consciously*. This means seeking a relationship with another, whoever it might be, so that both his own self and the other self are understood and recognized as subjects. The "law" becomes a way of life, a practical guide assisting him in his search, but it is no longer the ultimate reference as it was for the small child.

MORALISM: REGRESSION FROM THE MORAL LAW

Moral formulas such as the one cited above constitute a regression; reference is made to the law, and not to a person speaking.

46

We are back at the level of the child prior to his Oedipal crisis. Behavior is controlled by fear: "If you do what is forbidden, you will be punished." "If you are not smart, you will be deprived of dessert." "If you commit sin, you will go to hell." This last phrase is very significant; it was once proposed to me personally by an eminent churchman as the last word in moral education (which, by the way, was reduced to sexual problems).

After two thousand years it is extraordinary how we have reverted to looking upon the "law" as a transcendent absolute and God as a menacing policeman of sorts whose role and intention it is to assure compliance with the law. And no one can escape from this policeman, since, as we know, he "sees everything." Dr. Berge notes that such an attitude is simplistic, implying the desolate conviction that the "policeman" represents the unique moral principle of humanity.

By formulating morality in this fashion we are in effect recommending as the human ideal the affective reactions of a two- or three-year-old. It may indeed seem paradoxical, but this is precisely what has been proposed. We are tempted to ask how such a formula can possibly represent the primordial fear and panic we feel in the face of the indefinite and mysterious demands of life and our encounters with other persons. For we most definitely are concerned with fear or, if you will, anguish. This brings up the ambiguity of the second reference mentioned in the manual, the subjective reference called conscience.

There is no more confusing notion than that of conscience. By it we understand one's reflexive knowledge of himself as agent and decision-maker. The expression "my conscience tells me . . ." infers that my conscience is distinct from myself. Now, within the framework of psychology there might be some truth to the notion; there could be a foreign but menacing and demanding entity inside us which functions like a built-in director. Psychology calls it the superego. Throughout the prerational period of his development, the child acts—or vaguely tries to act—on the basis of interior sanctions that have accumulated in the course of his facing life. His "living dynamism"—an expression I prefer to "instincts" and "drives"—is undetermined at the beginning. From the earliest moments the external world and especially the parental atmosphere provided by the mother impose direction, that is to say limits, on his basic life force. The child construes these limits as a network of "counter-forces" reflecting his personal anguish in the face of the unknown.

The expressions we are compelled to use in describing the initial reactions of a child may strike us as exaggerated or even fantastic. But precisely what happens at this early stage is impossible to grasp clearly and even more difficult to express. Nonetheless, modern psychology does offer an avenue of approach, no matter how profoundly it may disturb our customary reflections. It is no exaggeration that a child regards these first experiences as constant risks threatening his annihilation; he feels them purely as reactions. The first sanction transmitted from the external world he experiences as the possibility of life, and he grasps the breast to overcome his personal anguish in face of the unknown. Until he is five or six the child "conducts himself" according to this mode of behavior exclusively, and proportionately less as he grows older. He assimilates the prohibitions that come from without and keep him from foundering before the anguish of the unknown and possible annihilation. He has not yet discovered others to the point where he can engage in a real dialogue of question and response. Before he is fit to do this he will have to overcome the Oedipal crisis. This primitive way of behaving—this premorality, so to speak—can be transformed only gradually from "living or dying in face of the unknown" into an evolving confrontation with others in conflicts or alternating frustration and acceptance that permit the progressive formation of the subject's conscience such as he is. At its best this adult conscience can be described in the following manner: "Only I can be myself, and I exist only in my relationships with others." Therefore it is this relationship to others that directs behavior; the subject can choose a specific attitude from a variety of alternatives. His act, then, is a response to someone; this in turn evokes a response from others. Thus while the word "conscience," when it is employed in the theological manual *without explicit and continual reference to the other* in this intersubjective dialogue, does correspond more or less to the reality of concrete existence; it corresponds to the sum of the anguished prohibitions obtaining in the most primitive stage of our existence. It is not a conscience involved in a living relationship with other subjects, but rather a superego determining infantile "premorality." The reference to the "law within oneself" represents almost exactly what the pre-Oedipal child experiences.

Confronted with works of this sort, we can understand very well why psychologists are protesting vigorously. "Neurosis" consists precisely in the regressive persistence in the adult of reactional modalities of the infant he once was, modalities which must in time be resolved or bypassed. Thus such a teaching can only appear conducive to neurotic behavior. And it is particularly poisonous since it bespeaks a religious attitude which unbeknown to its perpetrators disfigures and betrays man.

The first page of the manual which we quoted above is already sufficiently clear in itself: there is not the slightest mention of God as a subject in relation to man, and conscience and law are both conceived in the most infantile fashion. But the message of the book only goes on to corroborate our first impression. Everything is presented in terms of "permission" and "prohibition," without further elucidation. We could cite any number of examples, but we will restrict ourselves to the following few:

> To kill oneself indirectly is *forbidden* in itself, but it can be *permitted* for a proportionally grave reason. This is why it is permitted to work in foundries, mines, glassworks, chemical factories, etc. In the case of cancer, blood poisoning, etc., amputation of a limb is *permitted*.
> Conjugal relations are *permitted* when they are carried out in view of the procreation of children or for another honest reason.

The logical implication is that we have to engage in a scrupulous consideration of minutiae. Confronted with the pressing problems that real life poses, the legalistic mentality seeks to adapt itself in a consistently closed and unsatisfactory manner to distinctions based on details and circumstances. This is the impasse revealed by the hypothetical "cases of conscience" that attempt to solve abstract cases by abstract principles. At the root of it all is a

49

legalistic mentality. In the paragraph devoted to the Sabbath rest, for example, we find a list of servile works:

Works of this sort consist of laboring, farming, sewing, shoemaking, clothes-making, building, printing, working in mines or in factories, etc. In certain regions custom *permits* shaving, cutting hair, crocheting, etc. It is likewise permitted to travel, to go by horse or carriage, to row a boat, to walk, even if this be fatiguing.

The epitome of casuistry is reflected in the section on the sacraments. We find a whole gamut of dispositions according to which it is *permitted* or *forbidden* for one to receive the Eucharist, various obligations with their subtle but necessary distinctions, in fact, everything which so profoundly marks the attitude of practicing Christians.

With regard to sexual problems the identical attitude is applied with scrupulous fidelity:

It is therefore *permitted* to take baths, to wash oneself, to mount a horse, etc., even if one foresees a possible pollution. In the same manner it is permitted to scratch an irritation of the genital region provided that the itching does not proceed *ex semine superfluo* and *ardore libidinis*. When the cause of the irritation is in doubt, scratching is *permitted*. If the irritation is slight, it is *permitted* to scratch even when the scratching may provoke slight sexual stirrings. But one ought always to suppose that impure pleasure is not consented to.

We read further about "impure touches":

Touching the intimate parts of another person (even if only through his clothing) is a grave sin if it is done without sufficient motive, whether the person be of the same sex or not. Touching less intimate parts of the body is ordinarily at most a venial sin if it is done to persons of the same sex; however, it is ordinarily a mortal sin if it is done to persons of the opposite sex. The only exception is in the case of a superficial touch done out of lightheartedness or pleasantry.

No doubt the author had the best intentions, but in effect what he has produced is material closely akin to pornography.

50

He has reduced the mystery of sex to its erotic aspect. No wonder psychologists are confounded; they know that this simply does not conform to reality. And finally we cannot fail to notice how lightly the word "sin" (a personal act) is used to designate an abstract and indicative value.

Dissociated as it is from the theology of salvation, the moralistic attitude is fated to end in a blind alley. Because there is no reference at all to persons in the true sense of the word, it must culminate in pure subjectivism. Other authors draw more abstruse, yet logically faultless conclusions from such thinking. They see the "law" as an intolerable prison that must be abolished if we are to eliminate effectively the anguish it causes. This gives rise to a "situation morality" that by an absurd logic ends in destroying the very foundations of the dynamics of behavior itself.

DIVERSE MOTIVES FOR REGRESSION

Is it really such an inscrutable mystery why contemporary psychology reacts with such indignation? The "monotheistic myth"—of which Hesnard speaks in his *Morale sans péché*[1]—reinforces the anguish of law by contributing a menacing image that is equally infantile. Under the guise of Christian morality the manual we are discussing contaminates the atmosphere both spiritually and psychologically. It has been the achievement of contemporary psychology to indict this noxious quality in public view.

The reaction was not long forthcoming. Proponents of a morality of law reject with ferocious pride the conclusions and the very existence of modern dynamic psychology. As deplorable as this condemnation is, in a sense it is understandable. When someone has painfully established from childhood his affective security with regard to the world and himself, he is bound to de-

---

[1] What Hesnard means by the term "monotheistic myth" has nothing to do with the evolution of biblical revelation in the prophetical line that attains its culmination in Christ. Perhaps this explains why this work was not placed on the *Index*.

fend it vigorously—even aggressively—when it is impugned as pride, foolish illumination, a negation or a regression. Unconsciously he may realize the validity of the criticism, but he is nonetheless unable to accept it. His fundamental anguish, which is the same as that of every man, is not totally resolved or clarified, and he does not permit himself to face it. We only have to watch a "moralist" of this type respond to a psychologist's questions; he is defensive, panicky, violent and thoroughly rationalistic. And beneath his rationalizing one can perceive a foolish and unconscious refusal to accept unavoidable existential evidence.

To describe how morality got this way, we would have to go into great historical detail. Nonetheless we can ask how we arrived at our present impasse. How did intellectual reflection, and Christian theological reflection in particular, succeed in completely isolating scriptural revelation from human reality? The manual we examined above very bluntly ushers this question into the foreground. But it would be rather naive to think we can explain such an evolution, since in accusing this or that particular movement, or in attributing it to the influence of some individual author or some distinct philosophical distortion we are apt to realize we are only looking for refuge in a skein of abstractions. It is quite evident how ignorant we were regarding a scientific knowledge of man up until the last century. And we would probably be genuinely shocked if we tallied the naive notions and taboos which undergirded the moralist's positions at the close of the Middle Ages or in the period of the Renaissance. Without doubt modern man is much better informed about himself and the world than were his predecessors, but he is obliged to look at his mystery in light of his own situation. What makes it more difficult is that he has acquired this responsibility in the midst of an age of more authentic uneasiness than man ever knew before.

Perhaps nominalism is one of the most influential philosophical movements since the Middle Ages that had a profound impact upon man's manner of reflection. And it is best represented by William of Occam. His point of departure is quite simple: every being in the world is radically isolated; he is independent and shares no relationship with other beings. Logically then, since man has no reference other than himself, morality cannot be explained except by an absolute, interior imperative. Extending this to the limit, one might say man arrives at utter absurdity. This postulate of isolation (which for Occam was a strongly pathological schizoid structure) considerably influenced the fact that this tormented period could not overcome the politico-religious upheaval of the era.

Then there was the Renaissance and its rediscovery of the opulence of ancient culture. The thirteenth century was already a thing of the distant past; the vital and audacious thinking of Thomas Aquinas had already been dissected—and betrayed—by his numerous commentators. Slowly and imperceptibly pagan thought substituted itself for the religious view, and "morality" became a rationalistic *mélange* of Aristotelianism, Platonism and Stoicism. Though it dates from early in our own century, our manual is an excellent witness to this evolution: man attains his final end through rational activity. In spite of beginnings made in authentic spiritual studies, theological thought has been sterilized by the long, abnormal development of pure reason. Everything has become a *thing*; virtues, sins, faculties have become "things in themselves" to be meditated upon as so many pieces in an intellectual game. The insoluble dispute about grace is one of the more striking examples. While philosophical rationalism resulted in the notoriously naive positions of the latter part of the eighteenth century and the scientific romanticism of the nineteenth century, moral theology, still a prisoner of its rationalistic categories, continued to develop at the same level. It successfully obscured Christianity and was the cause of considerable disbelief.

There seems to have been another factor involved, but in this case an eminently practical one. The teaching of morality was gradually sheared from its theological roots. Moralists developed the habit of explaining moral necessities without a genuine reference to their fundamental Christian source, which is revelation. Consequently sacred scripture, instead of being the integral source of all reflection, was itself dismembered to provide isolated aphorisms to corroborate statements whose origins were surely more questionable than those of scripture. As contemporary exegesis is making more and more clear, it was not rare that meaning was imputed to the scriptures that was the very opposite of the intended biblical message. Apparently there was a legitimate need for a "catalogues of sins" to assist confessors and penitents, and there was obviously a need to "direct" people in a time when temporal and religious activities were so little discerned. But due to a gradual and strange aberration moralists eventually began basing their reflections on such catalogues rather than scripture. Consequently moralists suddenly ceased being Christian theologians and entered a universe of concepts that excluded the very notion of authentic mystery. The same thing has happened in the case of our manualists, precipitating the impasse.

But curiously enough this all happened quite unnoticed, making it all the more difficult to admit the embarrassing situation openly. When whole groups no longer show any interest in the Christian message, obviously either religion is being confused with political power or morality is being preached without any connection to the message of Christ, or both. Moralists began to preach an abstract morality, menacing and closed in upon itself, a police ordinance promulgated in the name of a God who is elsewhere reputed to be all good. Morality has lost its vital rapport with the living word of the true God incarnate. Looking back at his behavior since the beginning of recorded history, man realizes that the level of current moral reflection is no further advanced than it was for pagans who knew nothing of the message of salvation. This same rationalistic regression even contaminates our regard for the Word and the preaching of his word. This "good God" more resembled a philosophical principle than a living person who would rather die than see us go unredeemed.

We can follow in detail the history of thought and moral theologies as they gradually regressed, and we can discern the currents of thought which conditioned that regression: the nominalism of the end of the Middle Ages, "Cartesian" rationalism, the decadence of theology in the eighteenth century, the loss of the sense of sacred scripture, etc. But we can go even further. We can investigate the individual and collective psychological reactions that actually occurred and what it is that undergirds those intellectual positions that apparently express fundamental affective tensions.

Clinical psychology permits us to consider this question for the first time and to press for an answer. It is equally new that psychology and phenomenology insist upon the primary importance of interpersonal relationships—what Hesnard calls the "interhuman chain." The considerable progress in thought successfully frees us from the constraints of abstraction and already hints at where our answer may lie. Considered in this light, the "moralistic" reflex appears to be a regressive defensive reaction against the insurmountable fear of a relationship with another that this other person—human or divine—is about to reveal. It is fear of another subject calling out to us, fear of the movement and the necessary commitment involved in life itself.

Each human being has his own unique reactions; but there are similarities in personal histories. Dynamic psychology demonstrates that from infancy every one of us passes through various thresholds and common conflicts (birth, the "anal" period, fear of castration, the Oedipal complex) and that we manage this journey in a more or less imperfect manner. There is nothing astonishing in the fact that certain "kindred spirits" do exist: numerous personalities who react alike and in common to anguish. They protect themselves by means of a systematic organization of defense, using articulated concepts like an unbreachable fortress. There is no need to "psychoanalyze" these collective attitudes, for the very reason that there is no such thing as a "psychoanalysis" of anything but an individual, someone living in a particular situation. But for the first time analytical experience permits us to explore this fundamental "fear" in search of understanding and an explanation.

THE MORALIZING MORALISTS AND THEIR FEAR

The first need of every living being is life itself. It is this need which in a sense constitutes him from the initial moment of his existence. Man is a living being. His need to live is expressed in human ways, both in his consciousness and in his conflicts. Therefore we can best describe it by a term that evokes both these aspects, namely *security*. Man needs security. This sentiment of the "power to be" stands as a function at once of the external world —as it is confronted—and the person's unique aptitude for such confrontations. The more one's personality is psychologically "consistent" and enjoys a fundamental security, the better able that person is to confront new situations without risking a total breakdown. Moreover, the situation that is most liable to put that security in question is an encounter with the *other* as he is, whether he imposes himself as another personal entity or forces himself to accept the other as a distinct subject.

Any other person whom I meet is as mysterious as I am myself; but he is not the identical mystery that I am. In my own personal history I have succeeded in constructing a sufficient degree of interior security that permits me to live. But this security is organized as a function of the universe I have already experienced and to which I have largely adapted myself by reducing tensions and conflicts to a minimum.

This other person has a different history, an experience that is not mine, a security elaborated in a different manner; he imposes his own universe upon mine. The question is whether I can assimilate that universe without renouncing my own and whether I am capable of accepting more sweeping perspectives than those on which I have already established my own security. The question comes down to this: Am I capable of accepting the fact that others also exist?

The other person may be like me. But even brothers can sometimes be so unlike one another as to be in effect strangers; in this event a confrontation is difficult if not impossible. It can also be that two persons who have lived quite different lives and who might be judged as very dissimilar, could find themselves very close by reason of similar inner experiences and thus be ready to understand and know one another.

Accepting another person's existence and taking note of his reality in its personal dimensions—which is to accept dialogue—represents a radical requestioning of one's already-established (or purportedly-established) security at that particular moment. Up to this point it may have been impossible to respond to such a challenge, to accept the other; it may be that I have blinded myself to the intolerable "other" who threatens me and against whom I have no other defense than my blindness and insensitivity; I may act as if he did not even exist.

Real life is composed of interpersonal encounters at diverse levels that shift from the transitory to the definitive: e.g., the anonymous clerk who sells me a pack of cigarettes in the course of my travels and whom I will doubtless never see again until we are united in him to whom I have united my existence.

If we view morality with scripture as our point of departure we thrust ourselves in a web of conflicting demands of personal encounters. "Thou shalt love thy neighbor as thyself for the love of God." This shows that I must take account of at least two others *all the time:* my neighbor and God. And my neighbor, according to the irrefutable teaching of Christ, is *every* human being I meet in whatever manner. There is no difference of race, class, culture, political affiliation, etc. If I wish to ready myself for the call of Christ, I must bypass all the "thresholds" to encounter the other person such as he is in his human reality, since God loves him as much as he loves me.

Let us recognize simply that this is a dizzying demand. What is at stake is my internal security; and while it will be upset continually, this is what fundamentally constitutes progress. It allows me to recognize myself as a "self," absolute in my existence, but totally relative; proud, but lowly; irreversible, but imperfect. My real security can be found only in a constant insecurity accepted as the inevitable condition of my progress in consciousness and relatedness. We must recognize that the affective maturity necessary for a person's arrival at a certain suppleness of adaptability is not acquired automatically by everyone to the same degree. This is one of the more cruel affirmations of modern clinical psychology.

We should not be surprised that there are groups that form "defensive blocs" against the real demands of charity. When these human groups are "Christian" they congregate about a morality of law, of the style formulated in the manual we have quoted, defending it ferociously against anything that reminds them of the exigencies of their interpersonal relationships—and that awakens in them the intolerable anguish of knowing their fortress is being besieged. This is exactly the attitude of the Scribes, doctors of the law and priests who faced Christ and his apostles, pitilessly sending them to their deaths because they would not conceal the fact that love is more than the "law."

Nor is it surprising that these defensive blocs confuse a particular social and political order with the kingdom of heaven. Another instance is the integrist attitude. These are the same persons who react violently against all evolution or adaptation to new situations. Their reaction commences as soon as their affective security is menaced at a level inaccessible to their own reflection. Representative of this attitude is the confusion involved in the mystique of fatherland or nation. These are the same persons who react violently in the name of a code of morality against the disclosures of modern psychology. In its extreme form—and this happens more often than we would like to admit—the same persons will perform real acts of injustice without any idea of what they are doing in the name of morality or "Christian civilization." How does this differ from criminal injustice of the Sanhedrin that condemned Christ to the cross? Somehow our awareness of past history is extremely tenuous!

If we are to believe these reactionary elements, psychology destroys all morality. "If the primacy of the law is weakened, then all is threatened." But just what is threatened, exactly? Even supposing that modern psychology in reconsidering the law (as a "meeting place" and not as an absolute term) slightly mitigates internal restraints, what are the "moralizing moralists"—to use Berge's excellent phrase—actually afraid of? [2] All their protests to the contrary, it cannot be a fear of "others being lost." It suffices to recall that personal salvation is a personal and mysterious affair between Christ and the sinner: it is not the observance of the law that saves us, but grace (Rom. 8, 9). Remember the Gospel scenes: Zacchaeus, the "good" thief, the Samaritan, the sinful

---

[2] In fact as we have seen the discoveries of psychology, though they question the value of *constraint*, stress more profound and vast moral exigencies by promoting interpersonal charity.

woman who dried Christ's feet with her hair? Salvation does not suppress morality; it transcends it. If the moralists fear that people will be damned, they are simply forgetting that it is God who saves; they lack faith.

I suppose, however, that a great many of them do have faith, do pray and hope. Their fear is simply not what they say it is; it has to be something else. To begin with I think it is a projection of personal anguish, suggesting insufficient affective security or a poor integration of certain aggressive or sexual drives. While the degree of the weakness may vary, in all cases there are a number of similar characteristics. We have many obscure zones in ourselves that we are afraid of. The important thing is not to dupe ourselves or for that matter pretend that fear is a religious sentiment found in faith in Christ. The moralizing moralists have duped themselves to the point where they resent all these things without taking into account God as he reveals himself. There is something very infantile involved here, namely defense mechanisms that are ineffective but erected on absolute principle. In point of fact they are fearful for themselves, without actually knowing it and without understanding what it is that they fear.

As regards the first aspect, I think their fear is aroused when they witness the disintegration of their particular legal structure of existence. It provides them with sufficient security assured *from without*, in lieu of a strong inner security. The more intricate the web of laws, principles and contracts, the more they are at peace. And psychologists are about to break the disconcerting news that real life is so infinitely complex and dynamic that this apparently solid legal structure is only an abstraction and actually resolves nothing. This provokes a panic more violent than one might expect. I personally know some who have had real neurotic crises; they were churchmen who could not consider questions of marriage in anything other than a juridical or canonical perspective without going into a rage.

Finally such people consider their very position in life—their identity—jeopardized when the moralistic structure of their existence is put into question. Their affective personality is so fragile that they cannot exist without a strong identification with a particular "social role" (in the psychological sense). This is where the "clerical attitude" comes in. If a clerical moralizing moralist is deprived of his role of safeguarding morals in the community, he no longer has the essential significance he requires; he is apt to fear annihilation. Little does he know that this is rooted in the psychogenesis of his attitude in the first place. While we can certainly sympathize with him, quite frankly his attitude has nothing to do with authentic Christian priesthood—all apparent traditions notwithstanding. The distinction between the notion of *priest of Christ* on the one hand and that of *cleric* or *churchman* on the other stems from long centuries of confusing spiritual with temporal powers.

In the time of the *Ancien Régime* in France, for instance, the clergy was a constituted body like the aristocracy. But not long ago Pope John XXIII remarked in opening Vatican II that with the exception of the earliest period of the Church he was convoking a council that was finally free of political confusion. I recall a bishop in a very "clerical" region of France who told me one day: "My good friend, the day we make our pastors understand that they exist to announce the Gospel and not to straighten people out, we will have taken a great step forward!" I cannot say that this has yet come to pass.

THE ANTIMORALIST FEAR

However, if the "legalistic moralist" attitude seems to be a neurotic defense against life, it has a complementary attitude which we call revolt or the instinctive and passionate rejection of all law.

One can "fear another" within the framework of an essentially infantile relationship, the "law" being the way of protecting oneself against the sense of annihilation that stems from the "demand" made by another. But we can also fear another in what we might call an adolescent manner—since the terms "adolescent" and "infantile" do relate to one another. The manner of the adolescent is manifestly one of "challenge, as a form of question." He reacts to "another manifesting his authority" through a second

60

stage of fear; this constitutes the normal adolescent regression to the very autonomy that is menaced, since his interior security—his autonomy—is not yet firmly established. So he says "no"; he "revolts." The expression "He is a law unto himself" expresses this very well.

The "antimoralist" attitude is explained by the very contradiction entailed in normal (and therefore transitory) adolescent behavior. The adolescent is looking for moral autonomy: the subject must try to lead a life of his own in the normal adult fashion. But he is caught between the fear of annihilation by the "law imposed by others" (from which his opposition stems) and by the even greater fear of his own obscure impulses and the "stranger within himself" that he has not as yet integrated into a dynamic synthesis. This is the root of his "anarchy," as well as of the almost obsessive rigidity in many of his attitudes. The adolescent revolts and is intransigent at one and the same time; we are tempted to say that he is a "moralist in reverse." He seeks to create *his* law, but since he has not as yet achieved his goal he reacts fearfully on two fronts: against himself and against himself in the face of others.

It will be only after he has integrated his "inordinate" instinctive forces that he will be able to stand within the complex universe as an equal of others and as capable of having his importance, autonomy and *existence* recognized as such. Having found the necessary distance, dialogue becomes possible, and law will become for him a personal rhythm, an expression of his liberty and his engagement in relations with other subjects such as he finds them. He will have overcome sufficiently the "fear of being blotted out," and the law—the meeting place with the other—will no longer provoke in him a systematic reflex of opposition, since he will no longer evince a *fundamental* fear of others.

All of this is overly schematic, and it would be interesting to analyze in exhaustive detail the original sources of this "fear of the other" which every human conscience must somehow overcome to live authentically. It would be especially important to show what profound links exist between primitive affective experiences and the persistence in the adult of primitive reactions to

61

these buried experiences. But that would have to be the subject of a searching psychological and systematic study and this is not what is proposed here. It will be sufficient for us to note the "phenomena of the couch" to provide experimental background for our study.

If the legalistic attitude expresses the infantile reaction of fear of others, the corresponding anti-legalistic attitude expresses a fear of the adolescent type; but both conceptions of morality are equally unsatisfactory for promoting human living. From the point of view of mental health, they both represent a grave danger of dehumanization, and from a religious point of view they represent a similarly grave obstacle to the progressive establishment of relations with the God revealed in our faith, that is, to authentic spiritual living.

In practice these two fears conflict, or, rather, they stimulate one another reciprocally. This is what happens when "integrists" and "progressives" grapple with one another. Such neurotic affective forces are unleashed that both discussants lose their critical abilities and descend to enunciating outrageously illogical statements. We would expect such a dispute in a family between a child of six and his fourteen-year-old brother; but when it occurs between men in their forties who are otherwise intelligent and cultivated, there is surely cause for concern. Is it possible that fear can drive Christians to such lengths—men who in principle have heard the word of love and the salvation of Jesus Christ? Modern psychology has intervened to provoke a realization of this catastrophic situation and to throw some light on possible avenues leading to normalcy.

If morality does not make man conscious of his condition and destiny as Sertillanges suggests it ought, and if it is not formulated in a way that will help him promote his own usefulness and that of whatever depends on him, it has to be rejected and a substitute found. Under cover of an obscure fear that muffles the voice of God and immured in rigid and rationalistic thought, that which we currently call "morality" actually betrays man in both his natural and spiritual dimensions. In fact there is no longer a morality to speak of. There is only incoherent murmuring going on within a closed world.

What is dangerous is that many people, seduced by what they know only confusedly about Christ, are turned away from a personal and explicit attachment to him because of the moralistic formula. The simplistic doctrine of a manual such as we have seen radically brings the matter to a head. It is no longer a question of "historical doubts" that provoke disbelief, as was the case at the beginning of our century; these have been resolved through the refutation of a number of childish notions prompted by the progress made in exegesis. Instead we now have to deal with more profound and insidious doubts: "If this is the moral teaching of Christ, it cannot be taken seriously."

Is it wrong to think that this legalistic moralism represents one of the more subtle and authentic manifestations of the mysterious "spirit of evil" which scripture describes to us as essentially intent on turning man from the voice of God? The Gospel shows the incarnate Word grappling with the legalistic moralism of his time, and it is in the last analysis pride in the truest sense that constitutes this way of life: "to attain one's last end" by relying on the rigorous observance of an implacable law of which a caricature of God is the guardian. Since it is just as opposed to human nature —such as modern science has permitted us to better understand it—as it is opposed to the revelation of God, this "morality" has become unacceptable.

II. A MORALITY FOR OUR TIME

CHAPTER ONE: *Changing Our Method*

We are often given to believe that legalistic morality is a throwback to the Old Testament. But that is not exactly so; put that way it is insufficient. It is certainly a throwback to the Old Testament but only *insofar as it closes in upon itself*—if I dare to use that expression—and refuses to accept the progressive development of the prophetic line whose culmination was Christ himself. It is the "Old Testament" of those who persecuted Jeremiah, of those who killed the prophets, of those who crucified Jesus, of those who do not want to budge from *their* way of seeing things. This is explicit in the controversies between Christ and those designated by the Gospel as the "Jews"; this is not a matter of race but of attitude. Jesus was Jewish by his coming into history; Peter, John, Philip, Paul, the apostles were also Jews. In whatever era it appears, this so-called return to the Old Testament is a fundamental betrayal of that interior life which prepares for and leads to the success of the Gospel.

When we speak of authentic Christian morality, we are referring to a dynamic mode of behavior that flows from that view of the world which revelation—achieved in Christ—can give us. Consequently we find its most complete expression and fullness in the New Testament. No one can know what Christian morality is without referring *explicitly, essentially and constantly* to what Christ said and did.

We have already seen to what extent moral reflection has been disengaged from its primordial and living sources. Modern psychology by the jolting shock it represents for many people acts as an alarm to avert grave danger and subsequent damage.

We ought to take into consideration the fact that for many centuries, at least in the West, the point of departure for moral speculation has not been the word of God, but rather a confused jumble of valuable, rational truths and questionable (though unquestioned) traditions; of correct and fundamental intuitions, and ignorances that loom large in the light of modern science; of elaborated reasoning on good and evil and on a multiplicity of taboos. When we think that Thomas Aquinas proposed in his *Summas* that morality was a study of beatitude and that all his thoughts centered around relation (*ad esse*) and its primacy, we are literally stupefied to read treatises or manuals of the sort we have seen.

Little by little we have arrived at a genuine error in method (which led to rabbinical procedures): isolated fragments of the word have been extracted from the living context of revelation and elucidated by a decadent Platonic philosophy which has long since become abstract and purely rationalistic. Add to this the laziness of theologians, the submission to taboos or to the authority of certain authors (accepted evidently to the letter!) and the disorganized manner in which the human sciences have been represented up until the end of the nineteenth century! If we wish to answer the call of God and assuage the anguished hope of modern man, we cannot afford to become guilty of these same errors ourselves. What we need is a change of method *from the bottom up*. We must deliberately separate ourselves from the routine of using rationalistic formulas, the tendency to reify abstractions and the legalism which is the net result of it all. To extricate "morality" from the rut into which it has settled requires that we have the courage to begin a work that is forbidding by reason of its seemingly titanic proportions. It is necessary *to create a moral theology* whose primary point of departure is the accomplished word of God, that is, the New Testament, whose language can be inspired by the fruits of scientific reflection. Modern science, and psychology in particular, furnish us with a unique occasion to meet the enormous demands a new moral theology will involve. There is an extraordinary *convergence* between the conclusions of mental health and the revelation of Christ. Both the natural light of science and the supernatural light of revelation enlighten man *in the same sense,* though to infinitely different degrees of clarity. The former discovers the psychology and social exigencies of intersubjective relationships and demonstrates that this alone is the first prescription for a better humanization of the world. The latter considers the dynamics of behavior within the demands of love and enlightens by the love of the incarnate Word the insoluble phenomenon of human failure.

It is this new *convergence* that we must utilize as a point of departure if we wish to make a positive and faithful study. Thanks to scientific psychology, "morality," in the style of the manuals, is rudely unmasked as a betrayal of man and the word of God. What remains now is to construct a Christian moral theology based on natural and supernatural truth. Certainly it will require much time and a great many men, but the work has already been initiated by authors such as Bernard Häring.

FOUNDATIONS OF A NEW METHOD

Right at the outset I want to cite a number of New Testament texts that have been provided by God himself to serve as authentic points of departure. It goes without saying that their import is crucial to the whole study of moral theology and cannot be either ignored or dismissed.

So whatever you wish that men would do to you, do so to them; for this is the law and the prophets (Mt. 7, 12).

And he said to them: "You shall love the Lord your God with all your heart, and with all your soul, and with all your mind. This is the great and first commandment. And a second is like it, You shall love your neighbor as yourselves. On these two commandments depend all the law and the prophets (Mt. 22, 37-40).

Mark 12, 28-31 and Luke 10, 25-28 are almost identical to the preceding passage; they differ only in editorial details.

> A new commandment I give to you, that you love one another; that even as I have loved you, you also love one another. By this all men will know that you are my disciples, if you have love for one another (Jn. 13, 34-35).

This is to be placed in the full context of Christ's discourse after the Last Supper.

> Owe no one anything, except to love one another; for he who loves his neighbor has fulfilled the law. The commandments, "You shall not commit adultery, You shall not kill, You shall not steal, You shall not covet," and any other commandment, are summed up in this sentence, "You shall love your neighbor as yourself." Love does no wrong to a neighbor; therefore love is the fulfilling of the law (Rom. 13, 8-10).

> For the whole law is fulfilled in one word, "You shall love your neighbor as yourself (Gal. 5, 14).

The two texts of St. Paul are brought together in 1 Corinthians 13, 1-13, which contains the celebrated hymn of love.

The first epistle of St. John should be cited in its entirety and be read attentively; but note in particular the following passages:

> He who says he is in the light and hates his brother is in the darkness still. He who loves his brother abides in the light, and in it there is no cause for stumbling. But he who hates his brother is in the darkness and walks in the darkness, and does not know where he is going, because the darkness has blinded his eyes (1 Jn. 1, 9-11).

We ought to underline here the fact that the Hebrew mentality and language do not recognize certain nuances in our current language. *Hair* means "not to love"; this is what we must understand by it, and not the positive sense of hatred.

> For this is the message that you have heard from the beginning, that we should love one another (1 Jn. 3, 11).

> By this we know love, that he laid down his life for us; and we ought to lay down our lives for the brethren (1 Jn. 3, 16).

70

Beloved, let us love one another; for love is of God, and he who loved is born of God and knows God. He who does not love does not know God; for God is love (1 Jn. 4, 7-8).

Though this selection is far from exhaustive, it does illustrate that the law is contained in charity and that love does not suppress the law but rather transcends, assumes and achieves it. Love commands the law. The supreme measure of good and evil is not the law—although it does have this role—but love. What this amounts to is that morality is made for man, not man for morality.

The authors are the apostles; they transmit the teaching of Christ; they are "inspired," that is, the Holy Spirit speaks through their words. Therefore no morality can be called Christian if it is not *explicitly* founded on a concrete investigation into the exigencies of charity and is not constantly referred to the teachings of Christ. A "morality" *that results in law* is not Christian.

Let us take up again the definition of morality given by the manual of *Catholic Moral Theology*:

> *Man must attain his last end by his personal activity, in conformity with the remote (objective) rule and the proximate subjective) rule of moral action: law and conscience. These rules are violated by sin; their observance is facilitated by the virtues. From this the division of morality in general naturally stems.*

From the beginning the reader is introduced into a perspective where there is no reference to God except a very secondary one, for what the author has in mind is not really a question of *Christianity*. In contrast we would like to give a definition of our own which provides the basis of an *authentic* moral theology:

According to the convergence of the natural findings of science and reason on the one hand and the transcendent facts of revelation on the other, man attains his happiness by responding with his whole being to the call of God, which according to St. John is love. It is by striving in every existential situation to recognize and love his neighbor in a manner that promotes the other and himself in an authentic and intersubjective relationship that he responds to this call of God.

71

When this remains unobtainable due to his innermost contradiction and the mystery of iniquity, in the last analysis it is his basic attitude of love in accepting the salvation of Christ through a personal attachment of faith by means of which he leaps over the insurmountable hurdle of death and arrives at the perfect intercommunication of the kingdom of heaven by adoptive participation (St. Paul) in the very life of God.

Morality consists therefore in studying the concrete exigencies of charity (of which the moral law ought to be one expression), namely our relationships with our neighbor and with God. This evidently also includes penance, as seen in the light of the Gospel.

Brief as this sketch may be, we do have to begin somewhere. Already we can foresee this new treatise in morality as having two parts: the one dealing with the demands of charity, and the other concentrating on the dramatic situation.

THE RIGHTFUL PLACE OF LAW

Before anything else we have to make a few considerations about the law. Now, modern psychology is castigated as suppressing law and moral constraint. This is a complete misinterpretation of the facts. If the logical conclusion of modern science is a rejection of the "morality of law" it is precisely because it seems necessary and urgent to restore law to its rightful place in morality and to give it its full meaning. Here it is quite simply a question of revitalizing the often foggy notion of the "natural law." The abstract and rationalistic manner in which it is habitually expressed no longer corresponds to the disclosures of modern anthropology. Neglect on our part will forfeit for us the very reality of the natural moral structure. Modern dynamic psychology and the new anthropology which it engendered affirm this structure in a much more vital way as a necessary support of the human condition itself.

What should we understand by the "natural law"? It is all that the human conscience can acquire of normative knowledge about man's own behavior without reference to another Word directly addressed to it. In other words it is that moral law which reason can elaborate. The expression in current use is equivocal. It evokes an abstract world of the reasoning mind, of conceptual constructs divorced from reality. To avoid equivocation it would be much better to speak of "conscious reflexive understanding."

A complete study of man's position in the world requires that the human conscience—both personal in affective evolution, and collective in the progress of civilizations—take note of the imperative dynamism which necessitates the human presence. The revelation of the word of God completes this study and relieves the fundamental anguish of the former's insufficiency. In other words we can say man discovers in what sense he has to orient his behavior according to a "natural law"; but in the last analysis it is God who reveals where this will lead him, namely to God himself through the adoption of grace. Moreover the first natural stage of man's knowledge of himself and his destiny is apparently an "implicit revelation" and an initial call to man's supernatural fulfillment. To restore the "natural law" to its proper place in reality it is indispensable to reflect on the evidence of modern psychology as it enlightens the progressive structurization of conscience.

We have seen in previous chapters the essential structural element which represents the "law," understood psychologically. While the animal directs its behavior at the immediate level of instinct through a spontaneous and somehow predictive process of adaptation, the situation with respect to man is radically different.

At birth the human individual finds himself totally distant from the world he enters. His adaptation cannot be accomplished except *through* a specific process of conflict, since the end result of his adaptation cannot be predicted in advance. A progressive and reflexive knowledge of himself and the world to which he relates is an indetermination that requires from the outset a study of an adaptive self-determinism, which is at first very obscure and affective, only later conscious and reflexive. It is a uniquely human process: man's unique way of "being in the world," corresponding existentially to what we call "liberty."

This dynamic structurization of personality is normally accomplished through reaction to and assimilation of the "word" of another, understood as comprising all symbolic expression whether it be unconscious or reflexive (such as gestures and words) or even eventually rational. And this "word of the other" is in fact the first perceived expression of the "law": "Don't do this; do that," with the implicit corollary: "If you do this, you will be punished." In other words one could say that in a certain sense the "law" is the first phase in the meeting of consciences.

As one story has it a married couple overly concerned with psychology found themselves completely baffled by the behavior of their seven-year-old son. He was enjoying himself on a merry-go-round and simply refused to get off, despite the entreaties of his parents. The parents, naturally, were at their wit's end, and yet they were not about to think of withdrawing him forcibly for fear of "giving their child a complex." They sought the counsel of a psychoanalyst friend of theirs who was also among the crowd. The psychoanalyst whispered a few words into the boy's ear, whereupon the child dismounted immediately. "What did you say to him?" the bewildered parents asked. "Oh, it was quite simple," the psychoanalyst answered. "I told him that if he didn't get off this minute he would get a spanking."

The child needs the "law" to give him a basis for structuring himself. Initially experienced as the "expression of the image that his mother has of him," law reflects his fundamental need for his mother's love. Afterwards the law seems to be "the word of his father," interpreted and transmitted by the mother. It is vital for him: first as a title to "protection" against the menace of the enormous and as yet unknown world, but also—and this is more important still—as living proof that he "exists," that he has a "value" in the eyes of the adults around him. (On condition, of course, that the "law" formulated by the parents is not a way of neutralizing the child to make him conform to a set of prejudices of which the parents themselves are prisoners.)

In this hidden progress, as we have indicated, the child upon entering adulthood will experience the "law" in quite another fashion; it will become his personal rhythm of expression, an expression of autonomy, his individual engagement in relations with the world and others.

From the psychological point of view the "law" is therefore an important mode of structuring the normal personality, and to say that the adult does not experience law in the same way as the child does not mean that he wishes to suppress it. Quite to the contrary, this means he wishes to give it its full import as a place of encounter with others, as the expression or condition of successful intersubjective relationships. At a purely human level this recalls the expressions of Matthew, Mark, Luke, John and Paul.

Having affirmed this, we now have to clarify what we mean by the word "law." It is a term which designates quite different levels of organization.

We ought to be aware that we cannot end in the infantile reaction of submitting to any imperative uttered in an energetic tone.[1] There is a type of "submission" that is nothing but a surrender; and if the man of the seventeenth century was unable to pass beyond this stage of passive obedience, the man of the twentieth century, who is considerably more conscious of the need for autonomy—and the fundamental anguish of his liberty—cannot afford not to progress.

When a "law" is promulgated, unless we want to descend to a level of sub-humanity, we have to ask who is speaking to whom, and why. It is not until we have answered these three questions as thoroughly as possible that our personal acceptance can be truly human, positive, intelligent and effective. We are speaking of a Christian concept of man in which the human person—the subject —is elevated to his full dignity. The fundamental respect due to the human person resides precisely in the appeal to his liberty. To

[1] From this point of view it is equally indispensable to recognize the authority who is speaking and to gauge his real dimensions. When a Roman prelate inveighs against something in spite of his notorious incompetence in the question, this is not the Holy Spirit who is speaking: it can only be his personal exasperation which cannot otherwise be expressed. The history of "documents" on psychoanalysis, for example, is extremely instructive in this regard. It is interesting to compare certain individual positions that are taken which resound with ignorance and prejudice, as opposed to official pontifical documents, which are infinitely nuanced and prudent.

my mind the encyclical *Pacem in terris* is explicit enough on this point.

We can illustrate the first "level" of law by citing a traffic regulation. You must not pass a red light; otherwise you will be arrested and will have to pay a substantial fine. Now, who is speaking? The political authority in its legislative role; it is the man who is authorized by the community in which I live to organize the practical existence of this community in the most viable manner possible. It is his role. I even finance this service when I pay my taxes. Therefore he speaks according to what he is; he has the right and even the duty to speak.

To whom does he speak? To me, since I am a part of the community, but obviously not when I am in bed about to drop off to sleep or when I am reading a detective story. His word reaches me only when I am on the street, involved in what we call city traffic. When I am walking, riding a bicycle or driving an automobile his word affects me personally.

Why does he speak? Apparently to improve traffic conditions, to make as safe as possible this particular form of human relationships. In actual fact this chore involves the enormous problem of good and evil, since what is good and evil if not some mode of behavior within the framework of living relationships. The entire problem of morality can be found here at one level of its expression. And this amounts to saying that in the domain of human activity we always need control and improvement; we have no right to expect a definitive stability that would permit the total abrogation of law. Man is so constituted that if we were to suppress law (and arrest) it would take only a few minutes before the existence of everyone would be menaced in his own proper rhythm. In the case of traffic, everyone wants to go first, or last.

By means of the law I understand how to play my part in this continuous dynamism of bettering (or not destroying) living relationships. So when I see a red light, if I am aware of this total

76

context and am truly *free,* I understand it means someone else *could* at any moment dash out in front of me. I desire his peace and well-being (just as I desire them for myself when the light is green), and I can ensure things by obeying the law. It is not the fear of arrest that stops me; I do not even think of it. It is only when I am not free internally that I need the presence of an arresting officer of the law at the intersection.

Now it may be that I am rushed and nervous and persuaded that no one is going to cross in front of me, so I "jump" the red light as prudently as I can, *being absolutely certain that I will not hit anyone.* Or perhaps I am distracted from seeing the red light until I notice the policeman. Anything is possible in the reality of human incertitude. I mean that this magnificent interior liberty that keeps me from fearing the policeman never fully exists in anyone. But that is another problem!

Let us remark in passing that this "level" of the law is purely conventional in its expression. We have chosen the traffic signal as an arbitrary example; any number of examples would do just as well. It is *necessary* that there be a law, but its formulation is *contingent.*

Passing to another level, let us take the example of the law of monogamy. Here quite another thing is at stake, namely the very substance of the law and what the formula indicates. Here there is no question of contingency. There are not several ways of being monogamous. The society in which I live legislates that I cannot be married to more than one woman at once.

The questions of who is speaking and to whom are answered exactly as in the case mentioned above. But we still have to determine why monogamy, as far as we know, is not a universal institution throughout history, though we find for example—at the time of Moses—very primitive tribes (curiously similar to modern Eskimos) for whom monogamy and the stability of the married couple were the very foundation of social organization. Solomon had an impressive number of wives and concubines, a number obviously excessive and somewhat legendary besides. It was only quite recently, and largely due to the influence of Christianity, that the concept of monogamy came to prevail in the West. The influence of the Roman world also played a role, since polygamy was un-known there and divorce was prohibited. It was only through more peaceful contacts with Carthage that the established Roman cus-toms were breached. Even in the Moslem world we are presently witnessing a striking tendency to evolve toward monogamy.

It is evident, especially in the light of modern psychology, that monogamy is a progression toward "humanization," and it is one of the principal factors in the normal personal development of children—in the measure evidently to which the couple is a psy-chologically monogamous *couple*. The study of the affective devel-opment of personality reveals that the more a subject seeks what we call his "maturity" (for lack of another term) the more he tends to establish himself in an existential situation with one *per-son* of the opposite sex and to live with that person in a stable relationship in which the other person is experienced as different and complementary, but equal in "value as a person." It is at this level that the specific dialogue of the couple is established.

When "law" forbids polygamy, this means that the authority of the community in question tends to promote a more human structure of sexual and family life. The legislator may not have this consciously in mind, but this is of little consequence. What is at stake here is a normative statement of evolution toward an ideal. This is no longer like the red and green lights; here the "law" indicates that what is best is at the same time obligatory.

We could ask why, in whose name, and by what authority such a command is given; and the answer is by no means simple. No doubt through questioning, reflection, and reasoning humanity slowly attains an increasingly more complex and clear understand-ing of itself and its condition. Ancient intuitions which are at first expressed in myths, eventually find their way into philosophy; they constitute an effort to progress in what we call "natural morality."

In passing we can remark that the diverse contributions of sci-ence within this last century cannot help but aid in bringing rich elements to "morality," and doubtless it will be a long time before we will be able to fully understand their import and subsequently integrate them into one thought. But it might well be that in the understanding man has of himself—and of the couple's demands—we already can hear God speaking *implicitly*.

We come now to a third "level," that of explicitly revealed moral law. This is what we currently call (for want of a better phrase) "Christian morality." Who is speaking to whom and why is clear enough: God is speaking to us in order to lead us to the perfect happiness of knowing him. But we will have to be extremely precise if we are going to avoid confusion regarding the law.

In general we can say that for Christians, or informed non-Christians, "Christian morality" generally includes the commandments of God and the precepts of the Church. Upon closer investigation we see that these "commandments" of God are reduced to the Decalogue, that is, the moral formulas of the book of Exodus (20, 1-17). The prominence of the Old Testament perspective is striking, especially since it usually formulates its ordinances in the form of prohibitions. Everything here is as if the positive note Christ introduced into morality remains unseen or is at most of secondary importance. The texts cited at the beginning of this chapter, and Christ's moral discourse contained in Matthew, chapters 5 and 6, are literally set off in parentheses and then disregarded. The standard formulation of the commandment is "You shall not kill." But for the Christian, it should be "Love your neighbor as I love you." Among other things this latter formulation implies the intent that others might live. The word should really be such as God's Son fulfilled it. And it is striking to see a Church dignitary make a declaration against euthanasia in the name of the Church, for example, and give as his reference the *pre-Christian* and negative formulation of the Old Testament "You shall not kill at all."

This is insufficient and an analogy will make it clear why I *forbid* my six-year-old son to do something because he cannot as yet understand the consequences or engage himself personally in positive actions of a human dimension. But I will advise my son when he is twenty-one to help him discover the positive demands of his situation—his prospects, his dignity as a man. These two ways in which I behave, though they seem to be opposed, are simply two different ways of manifesting my love for my son. In both cases I desire his autonomy and well-being. Moses spoke to the "man-child"; Christ speaks to a man who is supposed to be an "adult." Our "Father who is in heaven" is not the imperfect father, angry or authoritative, demanding or dictatorial, that I as a mere man could be anytime. Why do we not communicate God's word as he actually meant it to be understood?

The other portion of "Christian morality" is made up of the precepts of the Church. But here we change levels and in a sense we return to the level of traffic regulations.

Who is speaking? The visible authority of the visible Church; or to put it another way, the accessible normative expression of the temporal portion of the Church. The similarity here with the legislative body of civil government is unmistakable, although it is not a question of identical behavior. Now, it is quite evident that the addressee is everyone who—both individually and collectively—is or wishes to be a part of this visible, temporal and organized portion of the Church.[2] No one is excluded; in that it speaks to every human being irrespective of his social or cultural achievements the message is universal. It expresses the message of the mystery of Christ at the level of organized religious practice. And the mystery of Christ as we know it aims to achieve the supreme destiny of man; it must inspire man by reason of its unique supernatural dimensions, and therefore it is by no means restricted to organizing man as a political and societal being. Consequently its prime purpose is not—as some clerics would have us believe—to prescribe what is "proper" or "improper."

But to whom does the authority of the visible Church speak? Here we return to our comparison with traffic regulations. It is necessary to regulate common practices and organized existence insofar as they are expressed in explicit relations with God. This we call religious practice: the rhythm of the sacraments, fasting, abstinence, etc. Here we are dealing with the contingent, not with the eternal. The manner in which the common rhythm of the

[2] This visible and *organized* portion of the Church does not fully comprehend its own mysterious nature, but it is nonetheless absolutely indispensable that the mystery have an accessible expression.

visible Church is organized is only relative: relative to things, though obviously the *necessity* of an organization of some kind is fundamental (the important changes in the Eucharistic fast are to the point). With that said, we should be aware that the precepts of the Church correspond to a reality and rhythm of life prevalent at the time of the Council of Trent, or thereabouts. Many things have happened since the sixteenth century. Communication between peoples, the possibilities of intercommunion, the social structures, the daily routine, the level of culture—everything has been so profoundly altered that it is impossible to imagine what life actually was like in 1570. And to live in the 1960s according to "rules" corresponding to life in 1600 or 1840 is nothing less than absurd. The rules have to be modified to accommodate reality—which only goes to show how important such regulations really are. But we ought not regard them in a legalistic fashion or prefer the letter that kills to the vital spirit.

In 1715 there was no railroad, no telegraph, no industry. Everyone could plan his own Sunday, for instance, without regard to what was happening in other cities. He could either ignore what was going on beyond the confines of his own neighborhood or rest assured that *sooner or later* he would get word of anything of significant importance. But nowadays things are different. Engineers, pilots, bus drivers, doctors on emergency call, telephone and telegraph operators, etc. have their day of rest, but not necessarily on Sunday. In our age the world cannot simply come to a halt for twenty-four hours. But so what? Return for a moment to our earlier example. The law disallows that I double-park my car; in order to do my part in promoting the general welfare I obey the law. But it is certainly quite conceivable that sometime there may be important reasons for me to disregard the ordinance—of course with an eye to inconveniencing others no more than necessary. It is the *spirit* of the rules that we must seek and obey. The letter is there only to aid us, and in fact under particular circumstances it may actually do us harm. The letter can be so outmoded that it betrays the spirit and the original intention. The case of traffic regulations is a good example. Before the massive change in traffic conditions we were allowed to do things which are now forbidden, and vice versa. This is simply being faithful to the intention of the legislator. (By the same token, we could ask how many religious orders and congregations are faithful to the spirit—the intention—of their founders. We so often confuse the spirit with "traditions.") It is the same thing on another level with the precepts of the Church; we must look for the spirit and adhere personally to that spirit. When a forty-year-old adult accuses himself in confession of not going to Sunday Mass because he was ill, there is something wrong. It indicates a scandalously infantile attitude which strips the Eucharistic Sacrifice of its sacred character. That is more serious than "missing Mass." How is it that many "practicing" Catholics act in this way, thereby reducing the sacrament of penance to a magical rite?

Even sincere Christians apparently consider the demands spelled out in Church legislation more important than the evangelical counsel to charity and often behave as if they were completely ignorant of the law of love. The Christian in the true sense ought spontaneously to respond to the requirement to love one another above all else. But rare indeed are such cases! Knowledgeable outsiders are led to construe the Christian life as entirely Pharisaical. How many "pious Catholics" are nagged by the need to go to confession because they ate meat on Friday and yet have no qualms whatsoever about charging exorbitant rent of a young worker who has to do without dinner three times a week in order to meet the payments? This is where the "morality of law" has led us! And the teaching authority of the Church is not entirely without blame. We speak of the "law"; we remember the "law." But if we fail to see that it has different levels and fail to accord each level its proper significance we regress to a stage of infantile legalism.

IS A BIOLOGICAL MORALITY POSSIBLE?

Nowadays when scientific knowledge is developing at such a rapid pace, we have to be especially careful not to become ensnared in a double danger. The first is man's tendency to pass over "someone else," that is, to resolve everything by himself; this is the scientific illusion. The second consists in wanting to "demonstrate" faith and its mysteries by placing science directly at the service of religious truth; this is the far more subtle and more lethal illusion of "concordism."

At this point in our reflections we can ask: Can Christian morality be demonstrated as true and necessary on the basis of scientific evidence? It is not easy to say, since most of the evidence is so new. But it would appear that we cannot, at least not without making gratuitous assumptions, seeking facile "proofs" and drawing hasty and premature conclusions.

Again an analogy might shed some light on the situation. I find myself marooned on a desert island. I explore my domain. In getting the lay of the land I notice certain things (a peculiar arrangement of stones, ashes and other traces) that lead me to ask whether someone else is also on the island. My feelings involve a mixture of fear and hope. But *until that someone speaks to me,* until he shows himself directly, I cannot be *certain.* Furthermore, nothing can help me resolve my incertitude. I can only continue to ask the same question (or if it bothers me too much I can try to put it out of my head). It could be that this "someone" arranged these signs deliberately. But if he does not show himself personally the question will persist, even though, I grant, I have made some progress toward an answer.

Similarly we can look at scientific discoveries as so many "signs" that raise certain questions. But as soon as we pose the respective question, properly speaking we leave the domain of science. We *reflect* on what we have understood, and this is another activity of man's spirit altogether. The question remains: What does it mean? Is there really someone? It is even quite possible to read scripture without noticing anything but a remarkable resemblance between what is being read and certain recent discoveries, especially psychological ones. But the question still remains whether scripture is really true or not. We cannot be certain that someone is waiting to reveal his personal presence because it simply cannot be formulated in ordinary words.

This is what theologians call the mystery of grace; it corresponds to the curious passage in Matthew where Christ declares: "Blessed are you, Simon Bar-Jona! For flesh and blood (human experience without the assistance of God) has not revealed this to you, but my Father who is in heaven." It is a discovery and affirmation on Peter's part that Jesus is the Messiah, with all the biblical significance that name implies. The attitude of the concordists in attempting to demonstrate the "truths of the faith" is not only very naive, but it tends to deny the necessity of the intentional presence of the other and to discard the mysterious element of faith on the pretext of affirming it.

The more we deepen our knowledge of real man through knowledge in general and psychology in particular, and the more we study the revealed word of God, the more we can affirm the lack of opposition between them. Actually human knowledge and revelation converge. If someone speaks to me and I understand, he actually invests the signs I see with their full significance. On the other hand if he does not speak—or if I do not hear him—I can only progress in the knowledge of things I see for myself.

Take another example: when I look at a stationary globe I can never see more than one half of it and I can never understand it wholly unless somebody describes the other half. The example is less than adequate, but it does underline the *absolute* necessity of dialogue. This is a delicate area where language can be a source of confusion. Carried on for its own sake and exercised in a healthy way, a certain grasp of God is within the reach of human investigation. But this "recognition" in no way compares to that which is possible when God takes the initiative, revealing himself and initiating the dialogue of faith. Modern science can only provide us with a modicum of knowledge that does not contradict revelation and which, in fact, may even help us eventually understand it.

Let us take the example of neural physiology. We are currently advanced enough to say that man's cerebral constitution differs from that of other higher animals in only one very important respect: Man's neurons and their attendant connections are so numerous and complicated that a considerable margin of indeterminism, and therefore of things unforeseen, is apparent. We might be inclined to say this provides the physical correlative of what we call "liberty." But is it legitimate to maintain that this satisfactorily demonstrates human liberty, or that it supports normative conclusions in the moral order?

Let me give another example. Man's cerebral structure permits him, should he so decide, to use his rectal musculature in a manner quite different from its normal function; this is what the "Petomanes" used to do in traveling shows. They "inhaled" air and expelled it at will to sound various musical notes. No less a figure than St. Augustine himself in his *City of God* gave a picturesque description of their "act" in connection with human liberty. Are we to say this "talent" is good simply because it is a peculiarly human privilege, or that it is more human and good to be a Petomane? Obviously this is an insufficient criterion, although I can well imagine some moralist saying: "*Amplexus reservatus* is a social form of behavior possible only to man by reason of his sophisticated cerebral structure and therefore it is morally good."

If this is true of physiology, it is equally true for psychology. From present-day scientific evidence we might deduce a "mental hygiene" that indicates what is more favorable for the maximal fulfillment of the human personality. For example, it appears that the unity and stability of the parents is the principal factor in the normal upbringing of children. But do these undeniable observations of science actually constitute norms of morality? Can science discover norms for both mental and moral health? I personally could not. To my way of thinking the foundation of the imperative ("It is necessary," "You must") is lacking and has to be sought elsewhere. Knowing what particular form of behavior will ensure a healthy personality is not tantamount to saying that that mode of behavior is morally good. There is no doubt in my mind that our psychological investigations could indicate a dynamic call to fulfillment, but that in itself does not constitute the foundation for an incontrovertible moral imperative. I will admit, however, that the moral imperative revealed in scripture in connection with marriage is echoed to a certain extent in the contemporary norms for mental health. But I do not believe we can expect much more than that. Moreover, modern psychology discovers and describes the evolution of what we might call the imperative entreaty of conscience; this is an affective entreaty. (We have seen in passing the heavy burdens of legalism which maintain this entreaty at a primitive level of its evolution.) This call progressively permits the harmonious integration of its demands in a life of "relationships with others" that are satisfying for everyone.

But why must it *account for* the integration? As a matter of fact psychology makes no such claim; this king of judgment is entirely outside its competency. It is rather the result of a kind of philosophical reflection that takes into consideration many additional elements. For there are "philosophies" which are no more than personal systems of rationalizing one's own neuroses; the idealism of certain authors is a striking example. And while a healthy philosophical reflection, placed in the reality of life by constant contact with psychology and phenomenology, can surely discern the outlines of a "morality" which would be truly human, I am persuaded that such a vague discernment is radically insufficient. It can only lead us to contradictions and anxieties which it cannot resolve of itself, and evokes in us a sense of loss. Just as the human couple can progress and be fulfilled only when each spouse accepts the other in the other's own existence and listens to the other while carrying his own burden in dialogue, just so, there can be no complete morality unless a dialogue is truly established between men and God. There can be no complete morality except in the perspective of revelation; and this is the evangelical perspective of love.

CHAPTER TWO: *The Moral Life Is Always Lived in Context*

One day as St. Matthew says (22, 15-22), the Pharisees planned to test Christ. They sent a delegation out to meet him that included members of the Herodian sect, who were collaborators with the Romans. The group was a strange mixture of legal purists, disciples of the Pharisees and those who had compromised with the pagans. After having flattered Christ that he was not preoccupied with the pagans, they asked their question: "Tell us, then, what you think. Is it lawful to pay taxes to Caesar, or not?" They were not really interested in the answer. The question itself was hypocritical;[1] they put Caesar and God into false opposition. But the formulation of their question is striking. They ask "Is it lawful?" Obviously they are only concerned with the law and Jesus as its interpreter is asked to tell them whether tribute to Caesar is permitted or not. God does not enter into their considerations, despite the fact that they pretend their question concerns real persons: Caesar and God. The hypocritical element in their request—the element Christ refuses to address—is couched in the terms "lawful" and "forbidden." The true question would have been concerned with the correct relationship required between persons. Christ's comportment in this situation constitutes perhaps the most lucid indictment of legalistic morality.

Moral man is always a subject in an existential situation. According to the Gospel and modern science one cannot speak of

---

[1] The Greek root of the word means one who is an actor. A hypocrite, then, is one who pretends to play a certain part, and who attempts to pass off his role as something real. In this case the hypocrites who confronted Jesus posed a false question in order to elude the real question.

morality except by expressing as adequately as possible that particular mode of behavior that must obtain between two persons in order to form an authentic intersubjective relationship. This is the core of Christ's admonition to love one's neighbor as one's self. It is in direct opposition to what we ordinarily call "situation ethics." This latter is an affront to our Christian sensibilities and is the logical dead-end of the "morality of law." It is in effect a closed morality where man is conceived of so theoretically that he eventually finds himself totally alone among a vast ensemble of moral imperatives. Were he to find himself in a *subjective* situation where observance of the law is impossible, he would simply disregard his obligations. Not a thing remains: neither subject, nor law nor human reality. And because this situation appertains to conscience, such behavior amounts to suppressing the very notion of sin.

Morality is trapped in its own iron teeth. If we advance law as constituting the objectivity of morality, we end in pure subjectivism. The concrete predicaments of each individual are so complex and so unique that his confrontation with law as the ultimate term of reference eventually leads him into a fatal cul-de-sac.

Mr. Dupont is married. He is the father of four children. In his present dire straits another child would mean catastrophe. He knows, however, that the more he fights against his sexual desires, "the more insistent the temptation will become" and the surer it is that he will succumb. Consequently he decides to "resist" no longer. He has sexual relations with his wife and withdraws just before climax. (Actually in a case like this we cannot even say he had a sexual *relationship* with his wife; what he did was to use his wife to achieve orgasm—but this is something else again.) As a consequence of his behavior there are no complications. Viewing his situation subjectively, he no longer feels bound by the law. In fact, the law was his primary consideration; he did not take into account God or even his own or his wife's person.

However, if we consider that the objectivity of morality is constituted by the *presence of another* and by the demands of one's relations to the other, everything changes. We can no longer shrug off responsibility. Mr. Dupont finds himself in an individual situation which makes it very difficult, if not temporarily impossible, for him to give a full and adequate response to his wife; so therefore his behavior is *pardonable*! But he cannot forget that what he does must exemplify a living relationship both to his wife and to God. As we will see in the following example, strictly speaking the notion of sin can only enter where there is a real situation existing between persons, which is to say always.

From all points of view, therefore, we cannot admit that the ultimate objectivity of morality resides in law. That would be at once contrary to mental health and to the Gospel. The first and last *resort* as well as the ultimate reference of moral action is the presence of the other through which the subject finds his own proper fulfillment. Where it is a question of a "neighbor" or of God, that course of action is good for me that most favors my *recognition* of the other in the reality of his being, my "acceptance" of that other—and therefore of myself—in successful dialogue. This exigency of relationships infinitely transcends the law, which can be no more than a schematic abstract formulation of minimal value. The law cannot be anything but general and therefore radically insufficient to constitute the *ultimate* reference of moral action.

THERE ARE ONLY SITUATIONS

The following evidence is unavoidable, though by nature it is often the cause of confusion and even anguish: I can never *exist* except in relation to someone else. This means in effect: "I am never alone," or, better, "My very existence is expressed only in relationships." It is particularly in this second sense that I personally understand the aforementioned evidence; for it not only implies the former, but it goes further. I exist only because God calls me to existence, and on the human level I exist only thanks to my biological relationship to my parents and their unique relationship with one another.

It is this "twofold relationship" which constitutes me both in

89

my own existence (which does not depend initially on me) and in my autonomy (which leads me precisely to depend on myself in my relations).

I can exist only "to," "toward," "against," "with." At the same time only I can be myself—no one else can relieve me of this responsibility. This all means that I am myself only in rapport with others, and this rapport implies at once presence to others and distance. Were there not others I could not even be conscious of myself. Every other person is in the same existential predicament: he cannot know himself without others, either. In this latter case I am among those others. In fact in every encounter with another person I am "the other," as well as being myself.

It is impossible to conceive of a situation in which a human being would not be "engaged" in some way with a whole group of other people. They might be persons he has known, persons he has spoken to, even persons he might have long ago forgotten; but at the same time he does not know whether they have forgotten him; he does not know who has changed and who has not. I use this as an illustration. Actually I think it is impossible to describe adequately the infinite wealth of relationships that make us what we are.

Here I am alone at my desk, writing. I am overcome when I think about the various levels of consciousness and unconsciousness simultaneously present in the world of man. For me there are my readers—all the people I address in their interior, private world. Spontaneously I seek to express myself in such a way as to command their attention, to awaken their interest, to have them understand me with their eyes and their minds. This of course does not mean I am succeeding. But at this moment I live as a function of my audiences. They literally make me exist here and now. This attitude implies on my part a virtual engagement: what if my readers should write asking if they might speak with me? And suppose there are 20,000 of them!—And then there is God, whose word constitutes my major preoccupation. He, too, is a stimulant, the most important stimulant in fact, to whom I must respond in writing. But I also have to keep my editors in mind (without letting them become a preoccupation); I have to take note of delays, paragraphs, contracts, etc. There is also the anonymous person typing my manuscript. And if she is a young and pretty typist, I am sure some of my acquaintances would be shocked. There are the eventual defenders of "moralism" who will only be more aggravated by what I am writing.

There are my appointments for this afternoon; I think of them because I am looking at my appointment book to see if I will have time at about five to finish this paragraph. There is the man who runs the store on the corner. I think of him, because I know I am out of cigarettes. I will have to stop there on my way to the Church, not forgetting to ask the owner for news of his son serving in the military. There are some of my old friends from the faculty of theology; I must consider them, since I am attempting to respond to questions we raised together fifteen years ago. And that brings to mind so many other persons!

Whether I want it or not, it is a fact: everyone, every human subject lives about me *at this moment*, even though I am alone at my writing desk. A man "leaves all" and goes out to the desert to be alone, but he isn't alone at all. His departure establishes a new relationship, that of absence, which can be more intense and profound than physical presence. For his part the recluse might experience liberation, but his actual motive is open to speculation. What is he freeing himself from? Does his leave-taking imply a rejection of others? Is he at heart incapable of responding to the demands of normal relations, or in choosing this course of action is he able in some paradoxical manner to actually strengthen his bond to other people?

The people he leaves can also react differently. For some it might mean impossible frustration, a negation or refusal. For others it may constitute an attempt to reach beyond the present stage toward a more profound level. The absence creates a distance which can abet a reciprocal state of "objectivity," and thus a dialogue freer of constraint. But it carries also the risk of the dominant resurgence of imaginary thoughts, the "suppression" of the other and his replacement by mere selected memories. If the absence—or the distance—is a positive factor contributing to a greater knowledge, it is evident that the hermit who departs is, contrary to appearances, less and less *alone*. But if his absence is simply flight, then he will be more alone, for he will suffer continuously from the failure of his searching, since his "world of memories" is only a narcissistic quest without end and unsatisfying. When anyone declares that he wishes to become a religious in order "to give myself wholly to God" or "to be God's own," we are uneasy. For does this not almost explicitly constitute a rejection of a relationship with the normal human world? Clinical experience demonstrates the relative frequency and seriousness of such an inappropriate decision, and that is why I feel it deserves mention.

But a person who wishes to "leave this century" in order to establish a relationship to others that is more profound in terms of authentic contemplation is obviously of a different character. St. Teresa of Lisieux offers a striking example. In any event, whether it be positive or negative, the relationship of absence is a relationship to others, and the subject who does the actual leaving cannot fail—to establish through his departure a new situation with these others that will have its own exigencies on the human as well as the spiritual level.

WE ONLY EXIST IN CONTEXTS

The teaching of Christian morality, *including the "law,"* ought therefore to be a formulation of the positive demands of situations of which we find ourselves a part. At any and every moment of his existence, each individual finds himself engaged in a complex web of relationships with others. To be schematic, I will say that I am constantly concerned somehow with my neighbor and with God, with whom my neighbor in turn is also involved whether he knows it or not. What demands does this situation make of me in order that each of these three *subjects* be recognized and promoted to the maximum within this living relationship?

This is an important consideration, and sometimes we are apt to be misled by certain forms of ascetical language. I cannot "forget myself" for others or "obliterate myself" in their behalf. The fundamental, irreducible dynamism of my conscious personality is to seek my own being and my own fulfillment, even when this is expressed in an aberrant or contradictory way (suicide itself is a paradoxical affirmation of the refusal to "live badly," of this "need to go elsewhere"). At this point we rejoin the thought of Thomas Aquinas who sees as the purpose of human action the quest for beatitude (*Summa Theol.* I-II, qq. 1-5).

The first contact I can make with God is in wishing for myself what he wishes for me, namely my happiness. But it is in love that beatitude resides, since God is love, and we are called, as St. Paul says, to "know him face to face." Therefore it is in the quality of my love and in my relations with others that I will find my own joy. The less my relations with others are possessive, the more I shall be myself. Christian asceticism consists not in "forgetting oneself," but in losing one's possessiveness. But this is more difficult in practice than it may appear. If one "forgets himself," which is existentially impossible, what one actually does is project himself unconsciously into the place of another, while in turn the other is obliterated. Or rather one puts himself at the disposal of the other to prove to himself just how capable he is of forgetting himself. In this way people who have a deep desire to devote themselves actually become great nuisances, despite their faultless intentions.

If I truly love—as opposed to possessing—I am the first beneficiary. This holds true not only for this world of man but for the spiritual world as well. There are innumerable ways of relating to things that are far more enriching than possession. But when we speak of a relationship with human subjects, we are speaking of another problem altogether. We react to dispossession by uncomfortable conscious or unconscious defensive attitudes. The most striking example is the conflict that breaks out between a young man and his parents. If the youngster acts aggressively or with indifference and simply quits his family to lead his own life, the typical reaction to his supposed ingratitude usually goes something like this: "His parents have done everything for that boy; what sacrifices they have made!" But if we examined the matter a little more closely we might discover that the parents never ceased treating their son as an *object-for-themselves*; in effect they have "spoiled" him, with all the terrible things the word implies. And now when conflict arises they are bound to suffer because they continually neglected to *live-for-themselves*.

The remarkable thing is that usually in situations of this kind the relationship between the father and mother is itself a questionable quality. It often consists of a compromise, a sort of *modus vivendi* designed to avoid a definitive destruction of the relationship. A possessive father or mother, for instance, sees his child in light of his own marital relationship and more often than not takes his revenge out on him for a situation he cannot fulfill with his spouse.

A study of marriage failures shows to what extent a possessive attitude of one or the other of the parents—or both—destructively disrupts the family relationship. It is in dispossessing oneself of the other that one can experience that person in the inexpressible totality of his being. This is the only way anyone will ever come to know himself in all his dimensions and will ever know the beatitude of dialogue. One cannot know himself as subject except as he succeeds in recognizing the other also as a subject.

THREE SITUATIONS

How might we construct a treatise in *Christian* morality which would express all we have said up to now?

A treatise is something necessarily general and therefore abstract. We risk being carried along in a logical chain of correct ideas which actually are no longer concerned with real people and are of no existential interest. We also risk discussing virtues, vices, and liberty as though they *exist as such*, as entities. Platonic idealism is always prepared to do this.

Temperance in itself does not *exist*. It *exists* only in persons who have a temperate attitude regarding their own pleasure. Nor does liberty exist in itself. It is a specific mode of existence and the presence to the world of conscious existing subjects; we can say that God is infinitely free, or that he is liberty, because he is precisely this threefold perfect existential relationship of the trinitarian mystery.

How then can we state the necessary generalities and yet avoid at the same time the danger of abstraction and idealism? This is the problem that the modern world poses to moral theologians, and they are seemingly not ready to resolve it. At present the best one can do is describe an approach.

I feel it would be valuable to proceed by means of "situation types," probing very concretely the positive demands for interpersonal progress, which is charity. This would mean a radical departure from the method and plan of the "treatises on morality" of the legalistic sort. We can evidently do no more here than present a few of these situations.

I

A woman enters the neighborhood grocer's to buy food for her family's dinner. As soon as she walks in the door she becomes involved in a number of relationships contingent upon her presence here and now. But these relationships are conditioned in turn by another set of more fundamental and stable relationships, namely those of her family, the reason why she is here in the first place. In other words, the situation includes the woman, her husband, her children, and in the background, the shop and the other customers—and God, with whom each of these subjects is in an absolutely essential relationship of salvation and existence, whether or not they actually know him or are aware of him at this particular moment. The woman behaves in the best interests of everyone concerned. She need only take time to reflect and she would become aware of the assorted requirements of the situation. She will have to fulfill her role as wife and mother before God. She must take into account the tastes of each person and the possibilities of agreement, the costs and her ability to pay without putting the household in debt. She must foresee everything that will make the family dinner successful. (In classical language, this is called the virtue of prudence, one of the four cardinal virtues.)

The situation will last several minutes.

There is the grocer, his shopgirl, the other customers. There is the busybody who is taking forever to decide whether she should buy cloves or cayenne. There is the shopgirl whose fiancé is in the army but has not written in a week. There is the timid man who is obviously in a great hurry but who came in on the heels of our housewife. She must face all these relationships at once and accommodate the individual demands. As regards the busybody ahead of her, the best thing is neither to annoy nor contradict her; otherwise the situation might last five minutes longer, and two other people in the shop would be unhappy as well. A kind word is in order. It has a better chance of putting the woman at her ease and helping her to decide. Everyone will gain, even the grocer, who is already becoming irritable. In turn the grocer will be more cordial to our own housewife; in fact he will probably be more cordial to the entire group. (In classical terms this is called the virtue of patience.)

When her turn comes our housewife will try to be clear, concise and quick in making her selection. As for the other customers, a relationship has already been established between them, the grocer, and our housewife. The shopgirl is preoccupied and is not in a mood for conversation; our housewife should be unassuming (the virtue of discretion). In her relationship to the impatient man behind her, our housewife ought to excuse herself by shopping quickly and paying him the courtesy of a few friendly words (the virtue of humility).

She will go home unhurried. If she has forgotten to buy salt, no matter; what she has at home will suffice, and tomorrow is another day (the virtue of fortitude). When she arrives home she pours herself a cup of coffee—but not two, since coffee makes her nervous and her children on the way home from school demand that she be calm (the virtue of temperance). The meal is likely to be pleasant; her husband and children will only love her the more.

This is what it means to be Christian, and sin consists of *not bothering* about these things.

II

Mr. Dupont drives to the office each day. He enters a very complex world of relationships as he does. There is his family, still at home. There is his employer and his fellow employees. There are other drivers on the road and pedestrians. Mr. Dupont is being called upon in this situation to avail himself of all his virtues.

He knows when he has to leave the house in order to get to work on time (prudence). He is courteous while driving, and makes no foolish moves when he is badgered by a reckless driver (justice). When he parks near the office he is careful not to hem anyone in (justice). And on his way into the building he recognizes the doorman with a smile (humility).

In the office he is careful in his relationship with his secretary (temperance and fidelity). And he consults his employer on any delicate matters that are better decided after consultation (obedience and fortitude). And all the while his subordinates should find him clear, relaxed, attentive and cordial.

This is what being Christian really means. And sin consists in *not bothering* with these things. Even if Mr. Dupont went to Mass each Sunday and said his morning and evening prayers regularly, he would not be a moral person, but a Pharisee, if he did not live his personal relationship with God in the Christian manner described above.

III

Jacqueline and Peter have been married for several years. They already have three young children and hope to have more. Their love for one another is illuminated by the mysterious presence of God and by a hope stronger than their fears. But they know for two or three years the responsibility of another child would be excessive and would burden the family instead of promoting its welfare. They have thought out the whole problem rationally and have decided reasonably to wait (prudence), which is to say that they have been fully conscious of their relationship to one another and to their children.

Jacqueline is in the fertile phase of her ovarian cycle, and Peter is too much in love with his wife to use her simply to satisfy his own sexual desires (chastity). If Peter wants to master the concrete situation he will have to take into consideration all the subjects involved—including the three children who stand to be deprived if another child is intruded into their midst. His wife is virtually a mother. And if he insists on having sexual intercourse Peter will have to use a contraceptive—otherwise he stands to neglect his responsibility to the children. On the other hand if he does he would indeed "possess" his wife, without actually making love to her. By using a contraceptive he would be denying an existential dimension which is hers in this sexual act, namely the dimension of motherhood. He would be denying as well his own dimension of fatherhood.

For Peter this is all too negative, so he chooses to abstain, bypassing his desire because he is authentically in love. This will only be in his power because in every other aspect of their married lives he has learned to know and promote Jacqueline in her dimensions as a person and as his wife. This requires *all* the virtues. It also implies that one does not arrive at the perfection of these attitudes the very first day, nor does one persist in virtue without weariness and difficulty.

A GROUP SITUATION

The clarity of a study of this sort requires that we distinguish different aspects of reality in order to study them independently. Nonetheless we ought not lose sight of the fact that this dissociation is artificial. What we distinguish intellectually remains in reality profoundly one, moving, changing and complex.

We can therefore distinguish two broad types of existential situations: those in which we are individually engaged in some way, subject to subject; and those in which we are engaged as part of a group. In fact each one of us is vitally a part of many "groups" at various levels; we are never individuals who are totally isolated.

The situations we have studied up to this point have not sufficiently highlighted this group participation. The housewife at the grocer's was a member of the middle class, for example, while the shopgirl came from the working class. While this is a part of their relationship, it remains in the background; the relationship is not established on this basis. But there is a second type of interpersonal situation where my belonging or not belonging to a constituted group is exactly the point at issue. When I am confronted as a member of a group by someone who is a non-member, and confronted more or less directly, what are the demands of charity as we see them? And inversely, what is expected of me when I am not a member of the group? Rather than try to solve the problem abstractly, it is better to propose an imaginary situation that is at once concrete and practical.

My train is at the station; it is scheduled to leave in ten minutes. I am sitting in a second-class compartment with six other travelers. We constitute a group; each of us tacitly accepts the others as "being there." For any number of reasons the group is formed and reflects our collective sentiment that we are satisfied with each other's company. We share an emotional security that might be articulated in such thoughts as "These people seem agreeable enough. We will have a pleasant journey together. We have enough room to relax." But three minutes before departure someone opens the door of our compartment and puts his head inside, obviously looking for a seat. As a member of the group with its instinctive solidarity and togetherness, the "intrusion" affects me along with the others. Obviously there is room to spare, although any one of us might spread out adroitly enough to hide the vacant seat. By his interruption this eighth person radically questions the structure of our group and its attendant "affective security."

How am I supposed to act in order to promote the success of such an interhuman relationship—actually, charity in its proximate expression? The situation can be very delicate. On the one hand this person is asking for something that is not only possible but actually by right belongs to him. He would like a seat in our company, and hence with me. But there are also the others. I have been with them for almost ten minutes now sharing their sense of security. My choice of behavior will have to take the whole situation into consideration.

Evidently what matters most is our welcoming response. And I cannot dodge my personal responsibility. For my part I have to accept him as I myself would want to be accepted were I in his place. But what about the others? Quite frankly, I have no authority over them. So I have to arrange to welcome this eighth person in a manner that is tolerable for the rest of the people in the compartment. His acceptance into our group will *destroy* the equilibrium we have already established, and it demands that all of us find a *new* balance of agreement. No one can know in advance how things will turn out, because we only have a quick estimation of the newcomer and this is bound to involve a great many of our own intuitions and instinctive psychological projections. It is possible (as one of innumerable alternate reactions) that my neighbor to my left finds the newcomer extremely unwelcome, simply because he upsets him; the person across from me, on the contrary, might be delighted to see a new face because while we may be tolerable enough we are not very exciting company. But none of us really *knows*; we cannot sense everything.

Christian morality demands that I do everything to make the group accept the newcomer. This presupposes that I will not surrender to the tendency to do nothing. This signifies that I am sensitive to the relativity of human relations (no more than that!) and that I am ready to set aside, in a *general* way, a certain acquired comfort in order to give myself to the external demands that solicit my concern, which is itself relative. In other words this presumes a spirituality I must already have acquired elsewhere. I will behave in a way that will reduce tensions and ameliorate everyone's concern. At this level the law ceases to be of much assistance. I have to *invent* something entirely new; even if we were all to meet in the same compartment a number of years hence the present situation is absolutely unique. Before our next meeting we will all have changed, each in his own way.

Now, assuming at our next meeting I am the "intruder," the demands of the situation are altogether different. I have a *right* to the vacant seat, and the responsibility I have to myself is primary. At the same time it is obvious that I am disturbing an existing order among persons I do not know. In this case I should make myself welcome, rather than simply imposing myself on the group. I have to invent words on the spot, as well as gestures and an entire attitude, that will transform the situation into a *group-of-eight*.

This is what it means to be Christian, and sin is to *refuse to bother* about these matters.

We have deliberately avoided going into exhaustive detail, as this is a study in itself. Instead we only meant to introduce the reader to the innumerable concrete situations that daily solicit our conscience along the same lines: how should we act when we are members of a "group" and an "intruder" presents himself and makes a particular request? What should a mother's attitude be with regard to the young man her daughter would like to marry? What should the industrialist's attitude be who is personally identified with a specific corporation policy when the workers come and request a greater say in the operations? How should a citizen of a well developed nation behave in the face of a people seeking political autonomy?

There is a plethora of similar situations to be studied, not only on the plane of abstract ideas and general axioms, but equally from the perspective of personal conscience involved with other personal consciences within a group.

This brings us back to our fundamental question: what is the term of fulfillment which man discovers as the motivating power of his ongoing existence? In other words, are our successes *at the time* of interpersonal communication in themselves *sufficient* to satisfy the profound aspirations of the human soul? (Again we recall the somewhat disillusioned remark of Dr. Hesnard.) May man "admire" his successes, as ephemeral and imperfect as they are, or must he see to it that they are no more than avenues leading to the discovery of something else requiring the "collaboration of God" and which actually implies in its plenitude all men always and everywhere?

Christian morality can only be expressed as a work in progress, existential and quotidian, the authentic mystique that is the encounter with a *living mystery*.

With this in mind can we formulate a tentative approach to the moral "revolution"? Is it not necessary to change our method radically, to reverse our ordinary way of meeting the problems of the *normative* science of human behavior? Taking the *fulfilled* word of God and our infinitely more profound knowledge of man as points of departure, must we not create a new moral theology, truer and more demanding (which no doubt will frighten the moralists) than the "classical" (which is to say "dead") version? This is the work—that awaits living, breathing theologians.

CHAPTER THREE: *The Moral Drama*

St. John reports a very significant scene. The Scribes and Pharisees (intransigent moralists of the law) bring an adulteress before
Christ in order to bait him. The description of the "group reaction" and the almost "psychoanalytic silence" of Jesus suffice to
give this passage the ring of authenticity. But that is not all. In
this short account we see the confrontation between a morality
satisfied with law and the morality of Christ that condemns adultery in a way more profound than the Mosaic law. The perspectives are manifestly incompatible, and the reaction of the Scribes
and Pharisees is intolerably simplistic and elementary. And it is
significant that the Lord confronts them personally ("Let him
who has never sinned throw the first stone") and causes them
to leave, one after the other, crestfallen and disconcerted, face to
face with their own moral drama, beginning with the oldest (as
the sacred author points out not without a touch of humor).

For Christ it is a matter of not being satisfied with the law
alone. The believer must make an attempt to understand what it
is that the law introduces. What we sense in every passage of the
New Testament is that the law can do *no more* than introduce us
to the demands of love.

Up to this point we have been concerned with clarifying some
of the *real* exigencies involved in true love. They reveal another
sense of the law—that which St. Paul expresses with so much
force—namely the sense of the religious drama involved.

In light of the existential realism introduced by modern psychology, the demands of scriptural morality go infinitely (or rather,
indefinitely) beyond those of legalistic morality. Quite literally,
these demands are limitless. Love has no bounds. And the law is

never more than the minimal requirements of love expressed in a highly schematic and fragmentary form.

The question that another person poses by his very presence is in fact without visible limit. "What does he wish *of* me?" (meaning, of course, "What does he wish me *to be?*") is already enough to cause a great amount of anguish. But the demands of love that Christ indicates in the "moral discourse" of Matthew (chapters 5 and 6) are anguish-provoking in yet another sense. Let us admit it; if we place ourselves in this perspective and reflect upon our behavior, we have to admit that we have not yet arrived at this stage nor do we even wish to.

There are frequently situations that we cannot "dominate." The housewife at the grocer's; her husband in traffic; the traveler in his compartment—each is incapable of responding adequately to all these situations. Either intentionally or through lassitude we are *always* making blunders. We are always "lagging behind" the response that we ought to give to the innumerable situations inviting our concern.

This is a very general statement. It often happens that we fail to respond to the needs of a situation because of ill will, egotism, or because it costs us something. But it happens even more often that our recoil is based on our poor knowledge of *ourselves*. We can never have full awareness; we realize things only after they happen; we attend to things with an attitude that we sincerely believe is one of goodwill, but which is actually motivated by the anguished rejection of the other and the problem he presents. It is highly probable, for example, considering the Gospel account, that the accusers of the adulterous woman were happy to find in her a scapegoat that they could castigate in the name of the law in order to justify themselves and put themselves in such a good light that they need not confront their own consciences. Actually they were not concerned with her at all, but rather with the law in respect to her. It served as an alibi. And Christ, who is nobody's fool, throws them into confusion by confronting them with themselves. Everything we said earlier about an "imaginary world" and a "world of phantasms" is applicable at this point. If legalism permits us to create a satisfying self-image (as the Pharisee does in the parable), there are other attitudes that are only the spontaneous seeking of the other whom we need as well. In other words the relations to the other that we experience are rarely successful, upon inspection, and what success there is is always tentative and fragile.

If we abandon the legalistic attitude, if only for the sake of mental health, we are bound to be astonished at our own *inaccessible potentialities*. For we will begin to realize how we must develop our approach toward others in order to promote all of us in conscience and dialogue. We will find that this constitutes our real fulfillment. But we find as well what a mysterious inner contradiction impedes our success. The "written law," when it ceases to be a screen, becomes a way of meeting and a reminder of our deficiencies.

Psychology for its part and philosophical reflection cannot lead us beyond this point. But revelation, which is entirely centered upon the drama, presents the "supreme interlocutor" who is not the law, but God. It is with him, personally and collectively, that we must deal.

An authentic Christian morality would deal with the real situation of the man who is conscious of his drama with God as it unravels. It would not be a rationalistic theodicy, but rather a seeking of an ever more profound sense of the living word.

The second part would be a study of sinful man in his relationship with God (and not just his confrontation with the moral or ecclesiastical law). And it ought to be the conclusion and completion of a successful attempt to expound Catholic morality. "Moral" theology and "dogmatic" theology in their traditional sense ought to be explicitly reunited.

SIN, THE ACTUAL SITUATION OF MAN

First of all a study should be made of the first chapters of Genesis, not scholastically, but deepened by modern science enlightening the history of the world and man. The evolution of the living universe and human race, the evolution of civilizations and thought, the dynamic evolution of the individual personality—all these dimensions that science in the last century has placed at the disposal of our conscience can *permit us to understand* the first three chapters of Genesis in a more realistic and profound way than heretofore. This is not our intention here, but I believe it is useful to indicate where we have to begin if we want to devise a more general formulation of a universal vision of the world that is at once scientific and Christian.

For our own purposes it is enough to point out that we are concerned with a dialogue of love—entreaty and response—that while it does not succeed nevertheless must be attempted again and again. It is a dialogue that begins with the creative call and will be pursued and "repaired" by the initiative of God.

The nature of man (for Thomas Aquinas original sin is a sin of nature and is not anyone's personal sin; therefore it is at the roots of the *self* of each one of us) admits of a dizzying self-intoxication that inclines man to interrupt his dialogue with God in its first phase, *to be sufficient unto himself*, to stop at the first level of conscience, namely time. It consists of his rejection of adventure and his inclination to know everything, while dispensing with all mystery, and this cuts him off from the other. All of a sudden night falls; the unique liberty of the human race can be lived only in ambivalence: enthusiasm and anguish, marvel and catastrophe. All of scripture is, after all, nothing but the history of a reestablished dialogue through and within the catastrophe itself. This is the drama of sin and its resolution. The notion of *sin* is strictly religious and *mystical*; it exists prior to its inclusion in any "morality."

This is the theme of the husband and wife introduced by Hosea, developed by Ezekiel and so magnificently sung in the Song of Solomon. The love of God is not limited by human infidelity; it rather waits upon man.

The anguish of Job in the face of his incomprehensible suffering and destiny shows that suffering is not a "punishment" for personal acts. As soon as we recognize this, the simplistic concept of justice collapses completely. And this is the upshot of the Pauline doctrine of the law.

It goes without saying that for St. Paul the dialectic of the law is of paramount importance, and his whole attitude and adherence to Christ is organized around it. Without exaggeration this is the crucial point in the Christian concept of morality. In fact, despite all appearances to the contrary, the moralists empty it of almost all meaning, missing the essential point that would undoubtedly throw their entire legalistic mentality into doubt.

In a certain way, for St. Paul, whose texts provide the scriptural revelation in this matter, the law is only a place where we can encounter God. The "law" makes us aware of our misery, of our *death*, and thus precipitates our discovery of the grace of Christ that will save us once we are grafted onto him through faith.

Is not the supreme relationship we can have with God precisely the definitive recognition of Christ as savior and our acceptance of his presence with all of our being? How then can we qualify as Christian a concept of morality which is not implicitly and continually centered upon this achievement? St. Paul was extremely outspoken in this regard (Phil. 3, Eph. 2, 1-10, Gal. 3-6, Rom. 4-9). Two statements in particular reiterate the essential content of these texts:

No one will be justified before God by the practice of the law; the law can only give us knowledge of sin (Rom. 3, 20).

The new alliance not of the letter but of the Spirit, for the letter kills, the Spirit gives life (2 Cor. 3, 6).

Man's own activity is insufficient. He cannot definitely achieve beatitude except by the grace of Christ, something he can discover and receive only because the law makes him aware of his miserable conditions. Note the dramatic dialogue evoked by Paul in his own regard in 2 Corinthians that propels him toward the illumination of love (Rom. 8, final verses). This is far removed indeed from the kind of thought perpetuated in "treatises" on moral theology.

WHAT DOES SIN SIGNIFY?

If there is one word we tend to use badly it is surely "sin." It is a technical term designating a reality that is at once precise and complex, namely the concrete situation of individual man or humanity as a whole at a particular stage in their *real* relationship to a living and personal God. It designates a reality which is properly speaking *mystical.* To have sin mean anything else constitutes an unacceptable abuse of language.

As St. Paul says explicitly, sin is a particular mode of one's relationship to God, and the law is only one way of making our consciousness of it explicit. The law is not the term of reference. According to the Christian notion of morality God is not the "instrument of the law," but rather the law is instrumental in helping us discover our need for him. When we read, for example, "Adultery is a mortal sin," the phrase has absolutely no meaning. "Adultery" is an abstract idea, and sin is a concrete situation existing between two living subjects. One might as well be describing a cathedral in terms of its mineral content.

We would undoubtedly make the whole issue less obscure if we would restrict the use of the word "sin" in the pastoral context. We would do well to distinguish the notion of *sin* from *fault,* for, while it might seem conventional so far as language is concerned, it nevertheless expresses something quite fundamental. If we base our thinking on scripture we cannot use the word *sin* except apropos of a situation where someone is conflicting with *someone*: neighbor and God. According to St. Paul the law is made to make us conscious. And the conflicting situation consists in someone's refusal to engage himself totally in his relationship to these others. One cannot therefore in any sense accept the use of the same term to establish a general formula that is perfectly just but whose proper character is necessarily abstract. We must find something else. And the paradoxical aspect of the present situation is that we have such difficulties in making the proper distinction.

"Adultery is an act mortally sinful in itself" would be an even more equivocal formula. "Adultery is a serious fault" would be only slightly more satisfactory in my opinion, the word "fault" being at least as confusing as the word "sin." We will come back to this point a little further on.

"Adultery is a situation that in itself is gravely contrary to the requirements of love and justice upon which the conjugal relationship is based." While this formulation has the distinct advantage of expressing the moral nature of the behavior involved and underlining its importance, it is nonetheless abstract. It presumes nothing about the personal attitudes of the individual subjects involved. We have to remember that Christ himself formulated the elements of the conjugal relationship, yet while he did judge the behavior of the adulterous woman he spoke no judgment against her. Rightfully, then, we should draw up new formulations of those situations that actually contradict the call of God. While they will also be perforce abstract, if we approach the problem in a new, more existential manner they will nonetheless sufficiently clarify the occasions of sin for concrete subjects.

Let us return to the notion of fault. As such it tends to place the subject in reference to a law or a ruling which in turn ultimately refers to another subject. Here is an example from everyday life:

While driving my car to work I do something unlawful. A policeman follows me through several intersections, tells me to pull over and gives me a summons. He is surely a subject, but this is not the reason we are now talking at the curb; at the moment he is an instrument of the law. Our relationship is not of itself intersubjective. It could of course become so; each of us might be able to humanize it, I by recognizing my fault, he by trying to understand it. But it might just as well remain as it is; I might remain stubborn and he might simply recite the law.

We have confronted one another because of the law. And while the necessity of law remains above discussion, this mode of human relations is far from satisfactory. "Legalism" reduces morality to the same impersonal level. Contrary to the whole prophetic development in the Old and New Testaments God becomes a kind of transcendent policeman. And the notion of fault becomes equally primitive.

If the law in fact is experienced as the ultimate reference of human behavior, what it amounts to is a misconception of the transcendence of God; he is reduced to a servant of the very law he promulgated. This is the substance of Christ's reproach to the Pharisees regarding the Sabbath; as master of the law Christ transcends it.

By the same token we cannot "argue with" a law. There is no dialogue possible with a policeman if he is obsessed with the rule book. If I arrive at dialogue with an understanding policeman and escape a summons, it is because we have both ceased centering ourselves exclusively on the law—I was going to say "stop stumbling over" the law.

SIN IS A RELATIONSHIP

This leads us to consider our relationship to God insofar as we are sinners. Now, sin designates the personal attitude of a human being involved in a particular situation. If we are at all aware of the nature of our human reality we will immediately realize that this kind of relationship is constant. We always make a less successful response than we are capable of. Our most profound devotions are always like wormy apples, beautiful in appearance but not quite wholly in order inside. There are vast zones within ourselves where many things take place that we prefer to leave in reassuring obscurity. But the dramatic lucidity of St. Paul dispels the legalistic fog. "I do the evil which I do not wish; I am capable of wishing the good, but not of accomplishing it." This last consideration conveys the Greek rather badly; one should understand "accomplish" in the dynamic etymological sense of "achieve fully." Here we find expressed in the symbols of Genesis 3 the real drama in the "original mystery" that makes us vacillate on our own journey. The good that we do must be measured against what we could do; the discrepancy here is important. We can go so far as to refuse to engage ourselves in a situation that makes demands on us. This is our sin: to fail to respond to the demands of love. We spend our entire lives either not responding at all, or not responding enough or responding only indirectly. We are sinners all the time.

Such is the fact that emerges from psychological investigation and revelation. From the legalistic perspective it is insupportable.

But I say we are *sinners* and not that we are "at fault." This is an important difference. As sinners we are standing in a personal relationship with a saving God.

Two attitudes are possible: we can be blind to or actually refuse the salvation offered by the other, or we can profit from our consciousness of sin in order to acquire salvation more profoundly in an attitude of joy and gratitude. It is this latter attitude that constitutes penance.

The first epistle of St. John clearly underlines this: there is the "sin which leads to death," which is the refusal or rejection of the grace of Jesus, and there are sins which do not lead to death (1 Jn. 5, 16-17). In other words, we sometimes find ourselves in situations that are not important enough to tempt us to reject the grace of Christ. (For example, not returning to a wealthy person the dollar he loaned for my taxi fare.) On the other hand we sometimes find ourselves in situations that are very important and that provide us with an occasion to oppose ourselves totally to God or our neighbor: for example, serious rivalry with someone ("Anyone who calls his brother 'fool' is subject to hellfire," the quest for money and power over others ("Beware you rich . . ."), the mystery of sexuality. We note moreover in the thought of St. Paul that such behavior is evil *inasmuch as it is idolatrous.* Sin consists in adoring a false god: money, power, sexuality, etc. And in the last analysis it is an imaginary and false fulfillment of oneself and one's aspirations.

But these occasions of idolatry are not necessarily always experienced as such, nor is their significance always understood, accepted, and desired willfully. One can kill, for example, without having deliberately chosen to, or without having accepted its profound significance. Those of us who live in the real world and not in the world of abstract treatises do not always experience our sexual transgressions as indicative of idolatry. In fact Thomas Aquinas himself estimated that in matters of sexuality we are most likely to find the least malice. The current use of the word "sin" to denote abstract and general definitions of evil situations has led to serious confusion in practice. Abstract definitions and the personal attitudes of subjects are equated *a priori.* Modern psy-

111

chology illustrates that the study of the dynamics of behavior in a given subject has nothing in common with the elaborations of normative general formulas: it is a *different science altogether*.

What disconcerts and shocks certain moralists is the fact that this new science of the concrete, personal subject in action contributes evidence that is generally misunderstood. We cannot judge the *real* culpability of anyone. We can only take into account a number of superficial elements: so-and-so has done such-and-such a thing; he knows that he is the one who did it; he judges he was wrong and that he committed a sin; he asks the pardon of the Lord; that is all. His interior attitude eludes us entirely; even our own attitude is bound to escape us since even the courageous among us are never able to fathom completely the motives of their own acts. We need someone outside the human world to judge. God alone can judge (note how Christ judges: the only persons he judges severely and in public are those who oppose his message in the name of the law). At this point modern psychology and revelation intersect: in the last analysis no one can judge his own culpability: "Before God we calm our heart should it condemn us, for God is greater than our heart and he knows all" (1 Jn. 3, 19-20).

We are led therefore to reflect on what we ordinarily understand by "penance" and the perspective in which we place the sacrament that achieves it. Throughout the development of biblical revelation the idea of penance corresponds to a specific relationship to Yahweh, the living and personal God; it is a relationship by which one *returns* to him by responding to his love. The spouse in the Song of Solomon and the prodigal son are two wonderful examples. This relationship has to be revived continually, since we are ever vulnerable to the mirages of our transitory, human condition. The parable of the Pharisee and the Publican is significant. The Pharisee expresses his self-satisfaction, in effect telling God that *he has no need of him*; the Publican expresses only the searching uneasy concern that *is* penance. True Christian penance is dialogue, not a bitter confrontation with a law that cannot pardon because it is only an abstraction—as correct an abstraction as it might be.

Perhaps the most suggestive Gospel scene in this context is that of the sinful woman (not at all a "prostitute") at the home of Simon the Pharisee. It is St. Luke (7, 36-80) who tells us the story. It is another of the explicit confrontations between legalism and the word of God, who is there in person. For one reason or another we usually think that Christ is going to pardon the woman *because* she has wept for her sins. But actually the woman is weeping and ministering to Jesus in order to thank him because her sins *have already been forgiven*. The brief parable of this debtor gives us to understand that since her debt was great so is her gratitude for being forgiven. Note the explicit phrase of Christ: "This is why I tell you her many sins are forgiven her: *because* she has shown so much love." The terse translation of the Jerusalem Bible here corrects our general misunderstanding of the scene.

As regards the meaning of this scene and the explicit teaching of the Lord, I would like to quote the following lines of Père de la Colombière in his letter (no. 72): "It is certain that of all those present the one who most honors the Lord is the sinner who is so persuaded of the infinite mercy of God that all of her sins appear to her as but an atom in the presence of this mercy."

This New Testament perspective—the only perspective that can be considered Christian—comes as no surprise to psychologists. While it does surpass their own work, it in no way contradicts it. But when moralists ignorantly indict modern psychology and "diabolical Freudianism," it might well be because quite unconsciously they are afraid of the shadowy world within themselves, of their own misery, of the cross, of God.

A Christian treatise on morality ought to include a well-developed section on the continually renewed encounter between man and God called penance, on its important elements and on its visible sign, the sacrament. The term "confession" happens to be radically unsatisfactory, despite its current popularity. It designates only one moment of the actual encounter, namely the relating of sins. And as you will recall the penitent woman in the home of the Pharisee "confessed" nothing at all in this sense. But what is worse, the word "confession" leaves the door open to legalistic regression—sometimes a very superstitious regression at that, as every priest who has administered the sacrament knows. More important than relating sins is the initiation of a dialogue with God that begins to save the penitent before he utters a single word. The sacrament should be experienced as a love tryst.

With this goal in mind we might investigate how and when the current practice of confession was instigated. We could probe the mentality it implies and the reflexes it takes for granted. We might study the early Christian notion of penance as a relationship between God and the Christian community (although we are bound to find that there were many ways of expressing the certitude of the remission of sins). We might also ask how this penitential relationship was expressed in the Eastern Church; what influence did Manichaeism, Pelagianism and Jansenism have, especially in the Western Church?

This historical investigation is of primary importance; we would see at what point "Catholic confession" was contaminated by a number of unfortunate regressions. We would also see how the manuals of penance that were written for the rude, ignorant priests of the late Middle Ages gradually replaced authentic reflection upon the mystery of salvation, thereby severing the mystical relationship of penance and transforming it into a predominantly juridical event. We would discern the role of casuistry that apparently was called for at a certain moment of history, but which hardened into the legalistic system of abstractions that Pascal castigated with such spirited indignation.

By locating these deficiencies historically we are in a better position to discern them in the present and to excise them. They so influence contemporary practice that many well-intentioned Christians are actually repelled by the sacrament of penance, indicating that it fails to be beneficial for their spiritual lives. As if this were not sorry enough, in many places there still persist superstitious and archaic practices that actually reflect the social, political and financial (alas!) mores of the Renaissance.

What is called for is a theological treatment after the manner of Père de la Taille's work on the eucharist. And of course we would have to reject systematically the customary legalistic (or canonical) point of departure. The moment is propitious for the venture. In fact modern psychology is already denouncing the ravages of a method so alien to its scriptural sources that in effect it betrays them. Psychology and phenomenology orient man's spirit toward the study of living personal relationships. It would be a great step forward if "scholastic" theologians began to realize that adhering to a theology of relations means rejoining that true tradition of the Church they have involuntarily left.

From the psychological point of view it is extremely important to distinguish two radically different situations: the relationship involved in penance and the relationship entailed in spiritual counsel (note that the expression "spiritual direction" is entirely unsatisfactory, as it implies the relationship of superior to inferior and intimates that some "influence" is brought to bear upon the inferior—with all the psychological and spiritual damage this can cause). When I engage myself in the situation of penance the encounter between God and myself is made *directly*; on God's part it is expressed by the "certain forgiveness" assured by the priest's inclusion within the hierarchy and the historical succession of the priesthood. Which is to say that the personality of the priest is only of *instrumental* importance and concerns me very little; it is not he whom I have come to see, but Christ. It is not he who "judges" (not he *who justifies*), but Christ. The priest cannot judge me since he is only a man like myself. He can judge—and then only according to his ability—only if I come like the Publican to the temple.

The ministers of this encounter should therefore be imbued with the attitude taken by Christ in similar situations, and not by treatises of the sort we quoted. To give just a few examples: it would be necessary to study *what really took place* between Christ on the one hand and the Samaritan woman on the other, between Christ and the good thief, Zacchaeus, the adulterous woman, the sinful woman at the house of Simon, and indeed between Christ and Peter. We cannot see how the sacrament of penance can be viewed otherwise. Nevertheless how far away from it we are in present practice! What we lack is a methodical study of certain Gospel events where we can sharply contrast how Christ behaved with sinners and how he behaved with those who had nothing to ask of him, namely Scribes, Doctors of the law, Pharisees. Thanks to the relevant material provided by psychology and phenomenology such a study would be unique.

When I go to see a particular priest (or layman whom I know to be a profound and wise follower of Christ) I am not directly engaged with God. While he is surely present, as he is each time we gather together in his name, it is not God who listens or speaks. Therefore this relationship develops relative to the supernatural, but itself remains on the natural level. As such it entails the many affective reactions—conscious or unconscious—that emerge in the course of any interhuman relationship. It involves any number of psychological forces that could lead to confusion, or worse, to aberrant behavior. Every intersubjective relationship brings into play the participants' personal affective worlds at various levels. Therefore we might say that in this context the psychoanalytic cure consists in founding these relationships upon a single mode of behavior destined to nourish and elucidate whatever in the interior world of the sick person can promote his life and future adaptation. Which, by the way, is to say that confession and psychoanalysis are of entirely different orders. And because spiritual counsel steers constantly upon a sea of emotional reactions, one cannot be too prudent in its practice. It is not rare to witness, for instance, persons who enter the priesthood through the influence of a "director" or pastor who has unwittingly wed the candidate to his own personal desires. Another example would be a spiritual director in his forties prompting a girl of twenty to make a private vow of virginity. We are certainly justified in asking what exactly is taking place in the subconscious labyrinths of these two counselors.

The confusion that so often obtains between "sacramental encounter" and spiritual counsel uniquely complicates the latter and often falsifies it. If we are going to rectify the situation we will first have to make a systematic study of the relationship called spiritual counsel in light of the findings of modern psychology. In essence the studies already available on the patient-to-doctor or social worker-to-client relationship mark a beginning. And A.

Godin's book on the subject represents a decisive step forward.[1] On the other hand what we need is a liturgical and pastoral move to dispel the confusion surrounding the sacrament of penance and to reendow it with its true meaning. A number of priests are already thinking along these lines, but their task is bound to be an arduous one since the juridical and legal reflex constitutes our defense against anguish and it is not likely to be dislodged without a great deal of effort. But despite the foreseeable difficulties it is urgent that we begin.

THE NOTION OF CULPABILITY[2]

The study of the dynamic evolution of personality has established the importance and complexity of the affective reaction we normally call the "feeling of guilt." Its first origins are obscure and irrational. And this poses a difficulty that is almost insurmountable: how to express in adult terms what takes place at the level of a child's initial affective reactions. All our efforts are flagrantly inadequate, and our "Cartesian mentality" is so deficient as regards symbols that we constantly risk being misunderstood.

I have no intention of describing the child's first experiences in meeting the world around him. That would require a lengthy study of his relationship with the "mother object," the progressive elaboration of the image of his body, the unconscious and imaginary image of himself and the various "menaces" and "risks" the child is called upon to experience in order to find himself *as a subject.*

In order to eventually perceive himself as radically distinct—to perceive himself as a "self"—the child has to undergo a separation, or, if you will, an alienation; he has to undergo the experience of cutting himself away. The very law of life demands that each individual in some way consummate this separation on his own, permitting him to establish himself in his total singularity. But this does not happen without conflict and uncertainty, since the

[1] A. Godin, *La Relation humaine dans le dialogue* (Desclée de Brouwer).
[2] See the supplement to *La Vie Spirituelle,* no. 61, second quarter of 1962.

child is encountered by his parents at both the conscious and unconscious levels, and this latter is by definition obscure. The process is fraught with jeopardy. The child senses this danger and reacts to it; in his interaction with the other it is inevitable. It will cause him untold pain (these are the reactions which are too violent or too unresolved at the time and which constitute the "knot" of neuroses which might later require psychoanalytic treatment). For the sake of clarity we say—and remember we are using the language of adult experience in an analogous fashion—that the child can be gripped with *anguish* when he experiences the conflictual situation as the menace of "being absorbed" by the other (as, for instance, by his mother in the early moments of life). Or he might be seized by *fear*—which is quite different—when he experiences the conflictual situation as the menace of being destroyed, stripped of value or mutilated (and this principally on the level of sexuality).

I realize this language is open to criticism and is unsatisfying, but I only propose it as an approximate convention and surely not as something absolute.

I think we can say that the affective streams of the feeling of guilt are located at the level of these two primitive reactions of anguish or of fear. When the child "risks an initiative" he risks, in his uncertainty and his as-yet-incoherent seeking, the other's "absorbing him" or "mutilating him." At this age (and it takes place during the first days of his extrauterine life) the other is not as yet experienced as a subject of dialogue! Long years together with this dialectic of success and failure will be necessary to permit the child, later as adolescent, and finally as adult, to perceive himself profoundly as a subject in the face of the other.

It is hardly paradoxical to note that this attainment consists precisely in the mode of being-to-the-world which corresponds to the possibility of saying: "I am not a partial object of the other; and the other is not a partial object of myself. I stand alone when I act." This signifies that the "separation" is positively accomplished, and anguish or fear sufficiently surmounted. The expression "cutting away" evokes another expression, that of transcendence, which connotes a "separation on high." And it is surely with an impression of "height" that the child is confronted by those around him. For a three-year-old, for instance, his father is a giant capable of suddenly creating joy, anguish or fear. The child has not as yet acquired a reflexive distance in regard to what he senses; what he feels is directly a function of how his behavior is received by others.

For the child guilt cannot as yet be anything but anguish or fear. The "law" which recognizes desire while forbidding certain realizations of it is the occasion of guilt. It is only progressively and much later that the father, whose "law" is the word, will be able to be encountered as a subject who is himself responsible to his word. When infantile anguish and fear are overcome we will find new meaning for the sentiment produced by conflicts we cannot avoid. There will no longer be the egocentric "panic" prompted by some "menace to my personal self," but rather concern for harming the other. Once a fundamental affective security is established the adult faces his fault by experiencing the other not as a menacing entity but as *someone like himself* whom he has injured through some inadequacy or error in love.

In the case of fault (namely as a way of behaving that I have chosen which does not promote the best interpersonal relationship) my so-called "voice of conscience" reproaches me. But if I am an adult there will not be the former menacing sense of guilt; in its stead will be my sense of conscience. I will not reproach myself as being "culpable" but will rather reproach the wrong that I have done to *another person.*

In one sense the father makes his appearance in the world of the infant as a "transcendent entity," but it is indispensable that this absolute personage who is the father—or the parents who are always right—make himself progressively less absolute. Parents should learn how to appear even to their young children as imperfect, capable of faults and themselves in constant search of progress. Otherwise the adolescent is in for an inevitable shock when his parents fail as "idols," setting the stage for the brutal disappearance of any accessible reference for ascertaining values.

The child for his part also has to cross a number of thresholds. From the "transcendence of the father" the infant, and later the child, must pass to the perception of the transcendence of God. If his relationship to his father remains at a primitive level the transition will be more difficult. He risks experiencing God (whom we also call "our Father") as the menacing entity of his childish fears. As regards the consequences of his behavior he will remain at the level of the "sense of guilt," without being able to achieve the "sense of sin"—namely the living relationship with God as he reveals himself in scripture. If the training we give him is moralistic, as is all too common, he runs the risk of never discovering the Christian mystery. By forgetting what is essential to revelation, "God" will remain a strange composite of a menacing Father and a caricature of that menacing power we find in the Old Testament. The regression that takes place leads to an attitude just as pernicious at the psychological level as it is at the spiritual level.

The Christian sense of sin is the reverse of the feeling of culpability, that closing in on one's own obscure anguish from which there is no escape. The adult Christian enters a living relationship with someone who loves him and whom he loves. The "fear of God" therefore becomes what Thomas Aquinas strongly distinguishes from fear, classing it, according to traditional theology, among the gifts of the Holy Spirit: the stimulating, restless attitude which seeks to avoid deceiving the love of the other.

A man is not happy in himself when he hurts someone whom he loves.

But if we did not have "conflicts," these hesitations and repentances, would we be able to *hear the message of Christ giving his life to us?* "O happy fault that made us worthy to know such a redeemer," the Church chants on the vigil of Easter. Such is the culminating achievement of the *sense of sin* which is so diametrically opposed to the egocentric anguish of the feeling of guilt.

REFLECTIONS ON RESPONSIBILITY

When a normal person comes into the presence of what is not himself, he spontaneously enters into a relationship with it that also establishes his own identity. Having achieved an adult integration of his relational life—by which he constantly perceives himself as a subject—he responds more immediately to the solicitation of that existence confronting him. Even if it be a question of another person, the essential and unfathomable mystery of that other person will not paralyze his attitude. If he is a philosopher he will reflect on this relationship, seek to understand it and criticize his own response—that is, his acceptance—in order to enter into a more adequate relation with the other and to deepen his own subjective perception of himself.

The schizoid cannot freely enter into a relationship with anyone but himself. A deep and primitive anguish inscribed in his initial affective experiences as a child retards him. So if he happens to be a philosopher he will question relation itself, since this is what causes his anguish. He will question whether that which exists in full view actually exists apart from his own thoughts. He is not at all certain, and in an extreme case he is apt to affirm its nonexistence for the sake of his own reassurance. This is idealism. It opens the door to a "philosophy of the imaginary"—to pseudophilosophy, the more or less brilliant unraveling of intellectual autism. It results in incoherence and negation of dialogue.

William of Occam, as we have seen, bases his philosophy and theology on the initial negation of any real relationship between beings, and thus any authentic relationship between oneself and that which is not oneself. This curiously pathological attitude conditioned the "official" philosophy for centuries. The net result turns out to be a paradox: numerous "Thomists" are in fact adamant idealists, complete strangers to the essential point of departure proposed by Aquinas. One cannot even say "I" distinctly in such a paralyzing web of logical concepts. And the treatises of legalistic morality are the most striking consequences of the system. Everything is expressed as if all that exists were isolated consciences confronting law. The only beings permitted in the system are "beings of reason" that are "purely intellectual." The notion of responsibility can only be understood as juridical and obligatory in the absolute manner of a categorical imperative. It has no signification other than itself. It is the attitude of a small infant paralyzed by anguish.

The *Petit Larousse illustré,* a popular dictionary with a fine reputation, defines "responsibility" as "the *obligation* to answer for one's own actions, for those of another, or for a confidence." In this juridical perspective one answers before a tribunal or an administrative authority. The notion of responsibility corresponds to a certain basic level of social morality, namely the necessity of organizing existence in the least harmful way possible. Implicitly it bespeaks a rapport between the individual and the community of which he is a part, but it is surely insufficient to constitute a personal morality, let alone a Christian one.

To "answer *before*" signifies that there is no dialogue, or, more exactly, that there is a preoriented and artificial dialogue between a person and a reality which is highly complex but which is not a person. All one need do is to attend meetings of tribunals in important cases to understand at what point justice becomes a thing in itself altogether independent of morality. Some magistrates are such slaves of the law that they totally ignore the human reality of the persons they must judge, to the extent of giving rise to scandal or inciting contempt. The juridical attitude which passes for morality can only end in an impasse.

Suppose that before leaving on a long voyage I entrust a loyal friend of mine with a certain sum of money. When I return I *ask* him to return my property. He *answers* that he does not want

124

to, or that he does not recall ever having been entrusted with the money. But since I have a receipt from him I apply to the competent judicial authority and put the matter in its hands; I *ask* society to join in prosecuting my request through the pressure of authority. But it is always I who does the asking. There is a fundamental intersubjective relationship between the one to whom I entrusted my money and myself. Since I am *asking* something of him he has to *answer* to me. And while the tribunal that studied the affair recognizes the reasonableness of my request and is going to question my friend, it will do so *in my name*. He will be interrogated imperatively by a legally constituted authority, and he is going to answer *before* that authority but *to* me.

By the same token when society pursues a delinquent it makes a request in the name of the community (namely all the persons who constitute the community and are potentially threatened by his behavior). He is pursued not in the "name of the law," but in the name of persons. If on the other hand everyone regards juridical authority as an absolute, only one party of the dispute remains, and the intersubjective relationship which provoked the dispute is in fact cancelled. There is no longer anyone present; the whole affair has devolved into a game played by dupes of a law that has become an all-powerful abstraction.

"Respond"—the root of the word "responsible"—designates an essentially intersubjective attitude: I respond to something asked of me. And if no one addresses me, there is no sense in my responding. Now, real life is nothing but a world of solicitations that have me as their object, or, better, as their subject, since I am the person being addressed. The entire universe makes explicit and implicit appeals that recall me to human needs, through the more or less opaque instrumentality of the living and inert world.

Note how profoundly it changes the notion of obligation when we realize that when I answer *before* I actually respond *to*, namely to *someone*, either singular or collective. This is much more than obligation; it is the very mystery of the request of the other addressed to me.

But *can* I respond? Am *I* actually being addressed? Who is calling upon me at this moment? These are the questions we have to ask before speaking of obligation in the juridical sense. In other words responsibility in the true sense is not the obligation to respond but *the capacity to respond as a subject to another person experienced as person.* This is actually the focal point of modern psychology. Psychoanalytic treatment has as its purpose to allow the sick subject to achieve responsibility; the patient is supposed to become authentically autonomous, a "master of himself" in his relationships with others, a true subject. Inhibitions, unconscious emotional conflicts, deviations and fundamentally aggressive or sexual dynamisms chain the sick subject to primitive and unresolved situations, and these persist and are repeated consciously until a solution is found. Nevertheless no one has ever achieved being a subject in the full sense of the term. But analytical treatment, by helping one to be conscious of what is happening, to experience his past insofar as it is past history and not a present burden, permits him to be more presently *himself*, and assures him more clearly of *his* response to the many demands and invitations of life.

In the clinical reality of successful therapy, and in all the perspectives which the Freudian discoveries have opened (in the domain of education, for example) we can say quite formally that modern psychology has lent considerable impetus toward moral human progress.

This proves—not in a mathematical or metaphysical way, but in the manner of the human sciences—that responsibility, the capacity to respond personally, is the highest instance of normal human functioning. This is the ultimate aspect of the psychological evolution of the human being, namely the possibility of realizing himself as a distinct and responsible person in interpersonal confrontations.

To request something means more than simply expressing a particular need or desire; when I request something I am in effect recognizing the other as capable of granting what I ask. If I am in a forest near a stream and am thirsty I simply take water. If there are only houses around I knock and ask: "Would you please give me a glass of water?" This simple sentence bespeaks an entirely different world, that of encounter. The one who answers the door and I find ourselves in that unforeseen situation of personal response that is liberty. And we know from the dialogue of Christ with the Samaritan woman the mysterious depth to which a request for a little water can lead us.

It is at this level that we recognize the difference between training and education. Training consists in creating conditioned reflexes that are more or less complex but which tend to make the behavior of the trained animal conform to our own wishes. Education, on the other hand, consists in formulating requests, that is, in evoking personal response.

When we ask a child to behave in a particular manner, we expect something more than a conditioned reflex: we expect *consent*, that is, a personal engagement, a response that is truly his. When education is reduced to training, what happens more often than we would like to think is that the child, not being an animal, is forced up against situations of conflict, inhibition and neurosis. To be human and normal, education ought to be a call for personal response from the child, well before verbal language is acquired. For there is a "pre-verbal" language. Education in propriety—for instance the appeal for personal control of the sphincter muscles—is a clear example. One *trains* a cat to be "house broken"; by training we can arrange it such that the cat's bowel pressure precipitates reactions that will make it leave the house. But for the child there must be a completely different approach. Direct psychological observation, such as the analytical exploration of unconscious traces, indicates that quite early the child has what might be termed an obscure sense of his responsibility.

From this period, however primitive, the child who has an emotional consciousness of himself in his first six or eight months of life reacts to the educative efforts of those around him by attempting to *respond to a request*—at his own level, obviously. It is his problem to conform to the wishes of his mother so that he does not lose her love in some way. When he begins to realize what is asked of him, which is to control his bowels, his first gesture is to offer her the product of his personal activity, literally speaking. Here at the level of a primitive activity is one of the first instances of authentic responsibility, that is, of an exchange with the human world about him and, principally, with his mother. The psychopathological clinic demonstrates how the poorly-resolved conflicts from this "anal" period can much later compromise one's consciousness of himself in his relations to others.

In the light of modern psychology, education ought progressively to lead the child to respond personally without anguish and without "flight." All prohibitions, injunctions and necessary sanctions should serve this purpose. The normal adult should be able to recognize his behavior in these relationships with others as his own, even if his behavior happens to be *culpable*, that is to say, regressive with regard to certain particular human demands.

What constantly falsifies our outlook is the fact that we tend to identify the notion of *responsibility* with that of *culpability*. This mistake is the logical consequence of the current juridical concept. To be a Christian man—from the psychological point of view—it is as necessary to realize and assume responsibility as it is *impossible* to evaluate exactly one's own culpability. "Only God knows everything," says St. John. As soon as we make the impossible equation, the moralistic prison closes upon us. We are judged before we have a chance to speak in our own behalf. If each time that I am responsible for a bad act I am totally culpable for the same act *ipso facto*, then I can only be condemned. In order to avoid such an intolerable situation our first reaction is to flee all responsibility. The child who is surprised while stealing from the cookie jar cries: "I didn't take them; the cat did!"

An answer like this already expresses the confusion we are speaking about. In this case we should make the child understand that he should not be afraid, that we know it is he who took the cookies, that he was wrong in doing so, but for this he is not menaced with annihilation or, what is worse, with less love.

To be responsible is to be capable of responding to someone for what I have done, of recognizing what I have done as my own action in its proper proportions; I should be able to tell how well or how badly I behaved. To be culpable is something else again. This means being conscious that I have failed to meet the demands of a particular situation, thereby causing my neighbor or God to suffer for something I have done. It also indicates a specific stage in dialogue: how can I answer the demand of another, this very suffering I have caused? It is at this level that we can locate the classical notion of reparation. But the important aspect of the situation is the response to the demand of the other and not the egocentric and endless wallowing in my own anguish in the face of the law.

I

One evening I park my car in the street near my home. I engage the handbrake carefully and go home. That night while I am sleeping, the brake fails and my car rolls backward and damages the car parked behind it. I am responsible. I have to be prepared to answer to the owner, but all I can say is that I am very sorry for the freak accident—for which I am in no way culpable —but since it is my automobile I have caused the damage and my insurance will cover the cost of repairs. I cannot express a feeling of guilt, since I am beyond reproach.

II

A fifteen-year-old boy enjoys himself with his friends by jumping off the bus before it comes to a stop. Often, of course, his worried mother gets after him for this. One day, instead of jumping off in this dangerous way, he waits for the bus to stop. But the bus starts up again abruptly and he is thrown to the ground and his leg is crushed by a wheel. He wakes up in a hospital bed some hours later; his leg had to be amputated. If the first reflex of those around him is to shout: "You foolish boy! We told you this was bound to happen!" the boy is likely to consider his artificial leg an unjust punishment for a fault he did not commit.

This actually happened. Five or six years later the boy required several difficult sessions to resolve the problem. He rejected the amputation as an unmerited punishment, and this bothered him more than it should have in accepting a simple accident. Surely he was responsible, and if one asked him what had transpired, he would have to admit that it was surely he who had taken the initiative in descending from the bus. But it was important for him that others recognize him as non-culpable. It was necessary that those around him react quite differently, saying for instance: "My poor boy, you've had such bad luck and it is unjust. For once you weren't foolish! You were hurt and we can do nothing about it. But it was not your fault; we know that. Be brave. You will get accustomed to this quickly and realize it is not a real catastrophe, just a handicap, and you will even be stronger than the others because you will overcome a difficulty that they don't have."

When after the necessary conversation the boy can make this point of view his own, true to what took place in fact, he has profoundly changed his attitude to life and others. His moral life will no longer be falsified by the confusion of "responsibility-culpability" that burdened him up to now.

III

Mr. X is a homosexual; from his earliest years his affective relationship with those around him has been so disturbed that it was impossible for him to express his underlying sexual desires normally. This is not his fault, nor is it usually the fault of anyone because what happened transpired below the conscious level of even those people around him. Now this man is an adult and carries around deep torments. The sexual desires that he tries to repress often escape his conscious control. The more abnormal and regressive the sexuality, the harder it is to integrate into the synthesis of a free personality. When under the pressure of his uncontrollable obsession, he enters a public lavatory in order to find a furtive "partner." Is he responsible? Undoubtedly, yes; he is responsible for what happens. It is he who is involved in the situation. But is he culpable? He knows that he is doing something "evil"; he is aware that he is "committing sin." But at the

130

same time he deplores it; he is trying in vain to avoid this kind of behavior.

If under the influence of moralism he confuses these two distinct problems, his only recourse is either suicide or total escape from responsibility—thereby negating morality as such or his own morality. But if on the other hand he is able to distinguish properly, he will respond to God. He will take quite literally St. Paul's words to the Romans (8): "I do the evil that I do not wish." He will ask deliverance in the manner of the Publican: "Lord, have pity on me, a sinner," and know that Christ explicitly promised him justification. This is by no means simply an excuse couched in biblical phraseology; he is making no effort to escape from responsibility. On the contrary, it signifies that the sinner who accepts his drama is actually *justified* by the infinite grace of Someone's forgiveness.

From the psychological point of view the confusion that leads one to identify responsibility and culpability signifies the absence of the normal power to discriminate concerning one's consciousness of himself as acting. This confusion leaves the subject at the level of the infantile anguish of the superego—and this is a *pre-moral* phenomenon. Whenever a child acts he undergoes a "risk" and carries about the fear of losing the love and esteem that is so necessary for life and progress. The adult should be able to bear the uncertainty, the fear of failure, the eventual reproach that one has consciously "sinned"; he ought not fear annihilation. The ideal of adult personal responsibility is to be able to recognize one's behavior as one's own, independent of its value, free from anguish and without aggressive vindication.

From the religious point of view, the identification of responsibility and culpability incarcerates the subject in a morbid world of "fault." It is a world impermeable to the message of salvation. This amounts to an "idolatry of law," an attitude closely similar to the original mystery of Eden. The most difficult thing for a man is to assume his responsibilities and *simultaneously* to submit himself to God for *reparation* and for fulfillment. Christ himself clearly specified that he came not to abolish the law but to *fulfill*

131

it, that is, to extend it beyond itself into a dialogue discovered in the mystery of personal presence.

If we regard our existence as fundamentally referred to law, all responsibility will evoke guilt. It will be a matter of being responsible to a judge, which already indicates that we are somehow accused. (Kafka masterfully portrayed just such a trial.) But nothing is further from the authentic Christian view. In fact it might well end in the heresy of Pelagianism—already implicitly contained in the moralist definition of morality we cited earlier. It either mistakes or actually negates the nature of grace, the infinite love of God which alone fulfills us in our destiny if we so *consent*.

But if we regard our existence as related to the living God whose acting Word became incarnate in history, we discover—through the law as a *partial* expression of God—that we are both lost *and* saved, that is, we are responsible and humble.

From the specialists in the history of moral theology (such as Canon Delhaye, professor at the Catholic Institute at Lille) we learn that from the sixth century onward confusion existed between moral responsibility (I was going to say genuine religious mystique) and juridical responsibility before the tribunal of temporal authority. This is not likely to come as any surprise seeing how the confusion between the "City of God" and the "City of Man" has been perpetuated right up to the present. But in the period of the barbarian invasions a rupture became apparent that precipitated a reaction more pregnant with consequences than we are perhaps able to appreciate. There was a return to the mentality of the Old Testament, with its stress on the impurity of *things* and its taboos (regarding such things as sexuality, cadavers, etc.). Man returned to the terrible mentality that preceded the discovery of personal responsibility (see Ezek. 18). Since then it has been as if the prophetical line of the Old Testament that was fulfilled in John the Baptist and Christ—of such radical importance for the very life of revelation—never actually existed. Instead theological thought has been pursued in that atmosphere of ritualistic and legalistic immobility which produced the Scribes, the Doctors of the law and rabbinism. The interminable quarrels of the sixteenth and seventeenth centuries concerning grace and the conflicts between the casuists and Jansenists are typical of this line of thinking.

The acquisitions of modern psychology are forcing us to withdraw from the prison. We rejoin Ezekiel at the level where one person responds to another Person. This in turn recalls the anguish of Job in the face of the incoherence of legalism, the discovery of the transcendent mystery of the Other who is without common measure, the possibility of perceiving the incommensurate mystery of love that announced the Gospel from Hosea to the Song of Solomon.

The *Christian* question of responsibility can be posed anew, this time with a more profound sense of conscience than was ever available to mankind before.

FINAL REFLECTIONS

It is always pretentious to have recourse to sweeping historical perspectives and to appear to draw lessons from them when one is not himself an historian. Yet nowadays such practice is unavoidable; at every turn comparisons of this sort are being forced upon us.

Men of the twentieth century are dominated by the need for a sharper and more profound consciousness of their continuity and historical significance. The considerable development in the historical sciences (history, paleontology, archeology, exegesis) coincides with the discovery of what we might call the "prehistory of the personality," that is to say, psychoanalysis. To my mind this explains our logical reaction to the dizzying confusion precipitated by the rapid and almost unbelievable progress of science and technology. And although such thinking has become a cliché, it nevertheless deserves our fullest attention. For cliché or not these are the questions which—implicitly or explicitly—are sorely affecting the thinking and the life of our generation.

Unlike our predecessors of a century or two ago, we are at a loss to plot our position in the universe relative to the questions it poses. The "mystery of the world" no longer asserts itself in the same way as before; consequently social situations and the relations between men are of a novel sort. All men and all peoples are demanding adult relationships between autonomous persons.

While this is evidence of great progress, it also ushers in a whole battery of new difficulties. And although we can point to some undeniable successes, we have also suffered a number of shattering

137

frustrations. But above all it is an altogether new way of being conscious of the mystery of our own human destiny. From the very beginning of the race, man has felt a primordial uneasiness about some kind of "severance." The different mythologies, the early attempts at philosophy, as well as the more elaborate systems like Platonism and neo-Platonism, were always based on the irritating question that is insoluble and expressible only in images: What actually took place at the beginning that would explain why everything is going so badly now? The notion of a "fall," of "demerit," recurs repeatedly in different currents of human thought.

It is biblical revelation that suddenly clarifies the many suspicions: something did *take place*—at a particular moment in the past—between the human conscience and the existing someone we call God. What is now actually afoot is a pursuit of love—as the Song of Solomon recounts in allegory. There is the invitation, followed by our rejection and finally the perfect reconciliation accomplished through the infinite power of a love that calls each and every one of us.

But today when science and philosophy are intent upon new pursuits, when man has achieved a novel and more profound consciousness of the dynamic perspectives of his own mystery and anguish, Christian theology and proclamation of the word of God are still couched in the language of several centuries ago. No doubt herein lies the underlying cause of the great historical event which was Vatican II. The exceptional personality of John XXIII knew how to crystallize the uneasy sense of incongruousness and how to provoke the necessary requestioning.

We currently find ourselves facing a demand that has been renewed many times in the course of history. A movement is necessary if we wish to remain faithful to the Spirit. When it was necessary in the course of the first centuries of Christianity to elaborate an acceptable formulation of the revealed mystery, the various and sundry councils were faced with a similar dilemma, namely whether to retain traditional formulas or to seek new ones. In this connection the history of trinitarian theology is very germane. Each time, the "integrists"—stubbornly committed to the status quo—eventually became the "heretics" who were unfaithful to the living Reality. The "revolutionaries" on the contrary (Cyril of Alexandria, Thomas Aquinas) inspired the necessary leap forward.

Revolutionaries? Upon reflecting, the word is not exact. It would be better to use the less common term "evolutionaries." It signifies those who are at once capable of authentic fidelity to the message of God *and* to the current level of human discovery. These are the people for whom the doctrinal formulas are insufficient expressions of reality that have to be constantly up dated, constantly requestioned in a common effort to see deeper and deeper.

The categories and conceptual schemes of scholastic philosophy are inadequate to express the message of Christ and have it understood in the world today. But the inadequacy of what is curiously called "moral theology" (in spite of its complete isolation from authentic Christian theology) is particularly shocking. Modern thought can only admit as the normative dynamics of behavior—a "morality"—the expression of the exigencies of interpersonal coexistence. In a word, this is the psychological revolution going on in the area of morality. First of all on the level of interhuman relationships, but also on the level of transcendent relations with the living God. The most powerful expression of these exigencies is that of the Gospel: to love one another as Christ loved us. With the Christian vision we will not fall into the shadow of what is purely conceptual or imaginary, since the term of the living relationship is the Other and the others as they really are.

But when we reflect on the almost unlimited and indefinite depth of these demands, we are gripped with a fundamental sense of fright. All relation whatsoever—and we are always in some sort of relationship—demands a total engagement, total availability, in order that it be an authentic interpersonal relationship as a function of "him who is the Other." But since such engagement and availability appear both necessary and yet totally out of our reach we are apt to be overcome. Nonetheless this *is* the mystery of living reality.

One can well understand why some "moralists," gripped with panic in the face of these demands, look for refuge in the false

139

etiquette of "moral theology," in precise rulings and minute prescriptions of what is "allowed" and what is "forbidden." It constitutes a regression to the purely rational, to philosophy, to a version of pagan eudemonism. There one finds himself the master of things; one empties personal existence of its attendant anguish; one has clear ideas carved into marble syllogisms. There one resolves the perpetual contradictions of life by means of the nimble, abstract reasoning we call casuistry. In its extreme form it culminates in flight from all responsibility, the ultimate expression of defeat that is "situation morality."

The world can no longer tolerate this attitude. And those who have based their lives on the word of Christ that enlightens the human drama can only be thankful that psychology, by its cold, piercing light, exposes those rationalistic illusions which are the subtle refuge of pride.

For our own good we must answer the staggering call of charity. It is always new, always on the move, and always demands fresh availability. It is the only acceptable perspective of that presence to the world by which God solicits us. Do we have reason to expect this authentic moral theology of charity and hope in the dawn of our approaching age?